hollywood haunted

A GHOSTLY

TOUR OF

FILMLAND

hollywood haunted

A GHOSTLY TOUR OF FILMLAND

BY

Laurie Jacobson

ADDITIONAL RESEARCH AND PHOTOS BY

Marc Wanamaker

DESIGN

The Fibonacci Design Group

ANGEL CITY PRESS

SANTA MONICA
1994

ANGEL CITY PRESS, INC.
PMB 880 — 2118 Wilshire Boulevard
Santa Monica, California 90403
www.angelcitypress.com

First published in hardcover in 1994 by Angel City Press
Paperback edition 1999
Copyright©1999 by Laurie Jacobson and Marc Wanamaker
Cover photograph of the Hollywood Sign: Copyright ©1993 Steven Nilsson

ISBN 1-883318-12-2

Printed in Hong Kong

Library of Congress Cataloging-in-Publication Data

Jacobson, Laurie.
        Hollywood haunted: a ghostly tour of filmland / by Laurie Jacobson;
additional photo research by Marc Wanamaker.
                p.cm.
        Includes bibliographical references.
        ISBN 1-883318-12-2
        1. Motion pictures — California — Los Angeles — Anecdotes.
        2. Ghosts — California — Los Angeles.   I. Wanamaker, Marc.
        II. Title
        PN1993.6.U65J23   1994
        133.1 09794 — dc20   94-33831
                                                    CIP

dedication

This book is lovingly dedicated to the unflagging spirit of my

parents Carol and Sidney Jacobson and the too-soon departed spirits

of Jimmy Drinkovich, Mike Friedman, Robert Nodal, Steve Tracy and

all my friends hurried to their next destination by AIDS.

acknowledgments

We are grateful to many people for their time and information, among them:

Julie Andrews, Pete Bateman, Jeannette Batton, Michael Becker, Pandro Berman, Jerry Brake, Corinne Broskette, Mike Caffey, Chateau Marmont, Blake Clark, Bob Codik, Barry Conrad, Douglas S. Cramer, Eddie Crispell, Marisa De Simone, Sean Diviny, Sean Dobbs, the staff of Larry Edmunds Bookstore, Eric Eisenberg, Lisa Fredsti, the staff of Grave Line Tours, Michael Hawks, Albert Heintzelman, Eugene Hilchey, Bob Hill, Jan and June Hokom, Hollywood Heritage Inc., Susan Hurlburt, Joseph Jasgur, Fred Jordan, Ed Karas, Ken Kenyon, Pearl Lasky, Andrew Lee, June Lockhart, A.C. Lyles, Tim Mahoney, Nancy Malone, Dick Mason, Scott Michaels, Lillian Michaelson, Mark C. Miller, Lisa Mitchell, Benny Montanyo, Tom Murray, Charles Oelze, Jill Place, Tiffany Peterson, LaMonta Pierson, Rick Rivera, Emilo Rosales, Peter Roulant, Karla Rubin, Art Satren, Joel Schiller, Richard Schnyder, Giselle Seibert, Jim and Melissa Sharp, Mel Sherer, Mitzi Shore, William J. Smith, Dwayne Soto, Dr. Barry Taff, Wes and Marnee Thompson, Jerri Thomson, Jack Warner Jr., Michael Yakaitis.

contents

introduction

My first encounter with a ghost was at Hollywood's Chinese Theater on a private tour with four other historians in 1992. I was the only one to walk through the area behind the movie screen, where once up to two hundred people waited to make their entrance for the live prologue before the feature film. Afterward, I climbed down from the stage and joined the others in the auditorium. Inexplicably, we all looked to the edge of the stage where I'd been standing. The velvet curtain hanging to the side was shaking violently. It seemed to be gripped by a pair of unseen hands that were jerking it back and forth. I turned to my companions.

"Do you see that?" I asked. They all did. I felt that someone was telling me I had invaded their territory, that it was meant to frighten me—and it did. I ran out into the lobby. I regret it now. I've been looking for ghosts ever since.

Left: Grauman's Chinese Theater, 1928

As Hollywood historians, Marc Wanamaker and I have learned a lot more than dates and places. The history of this town and the movie industry includes a fabulous nightlife, sensational scandals, dramatic suicides and gripping murder mysteries. We have collected these stories for years. Some we found to be only lore: Thelma Todd's ghost has never been seen near her cafe or in the garage where she died by anyone *we* could find. And Houdini most likely never even set foot in the Laurel Canyon mansion he is said to haunt.

Happily, we confirmed the presence of many Hollywood spirits, and discovered some new ones, but not without help. First, we enlisted the aid of Eddie Crispell, who has been psychic all her life. "If there's a ghost," Eddie told us, "I know it."

We also sought out Dr. Barry Taff, a parapsychologist who has examined more than 3,200 reported hauntings in twenty-six years. Many of those occurred between 1968 and 1978, when Taff served as research associate in the parapsychology lab in the Neuropsychiatric Institute at the University of California at Los Angeles' Center for Health Sciences. The lab disbanded for lack of funding. Since then, Taff has served as technical advisor on such films as *Poltergeist* and *Altered States*, as well as consultant to the Central Intelligence Agency, Federal Bureau of Investigation, Interpol and more. His most famous case was chronicled in the book and 1983 film *The Entity*.

"The one area of the paranormal that seems to be constant throughout the world is the appearance of ghosts and hauntings," Taff explains. "It's cross-cultural and stems from the very beginnings of civilization."

But what are ghosts? Why are they here? Why do some people see them while others do not? Scientifically, there are no set answers. Taff has witnessed ectoplasmic manifestations, balls of light, apportments—objects disappearing from one place and reappearing in another by their own volition—spontaneous fires, shaking rooms, bouncing furniture, unusual smells. "I know what we tend to call it, how we categorize it," he says, "but I don't know exactly what we're dealing with."

Spiritually, there are answers. Many believe ghosts are earthbound spirits of people who have died. Often, at the sites of great emotion or sudden death, there are reports of ghosts. The reasons spirits stay earthbound are varied. Some people, when living, don't believe there is anything after this life. When they find themselves, as spirits, still aware and able to move, they are confused and don't know where to go. And if one does believe in heaven and hell, it's only logical that a small percentage of spirits might get lost on the way.

Some spirits—like Clifton Webb's—are too attached to a place or loved one to leave. In the case of murder, the victim's spirit may remain seeking retribution, like the ghosts who haunt Bessie Love's home. In the case of a life cut short, like that of Sam Warner, the spirit may linger because of unfinished business.

The 1990 film *Ghost* comes closest to what many parapsychologists believe is the truth—that some spirits can materialize or move things, while some have not yet learned. Spirits draw on energy from the living to accomplish these feats. People who don't believe in ghosts give them no energy and therefore rarely witness phenomena. But fear is a very powerful energy, so people who are terrified often have more dramatic manifestations.

Eddie Crispell reasons that some people can easily tune into the frequency; others cannot. We don't know why. Many eyewitnesses in the book can describe the spirits they saw in detail: hair, clothes, features. Others saw only shadows. And two saw shimmering, jellyfish-type masses. The headless ghost of Beverly Glen is loving and comforting, while one of the spirits at the Comedy Store seems deeply malevolent. I believe in ghosts, am afraid of them and have been in the presence of some, yet I have never felt anything more than a cold spot.

The only common ground our ghosts share is their Hollywood haunts, but their shapes, sizes and personalities are as diverse as humankind. Now, isn't that a coincidence ...

Laurie Jacobson, HOLLYWOOD, JULY 1994

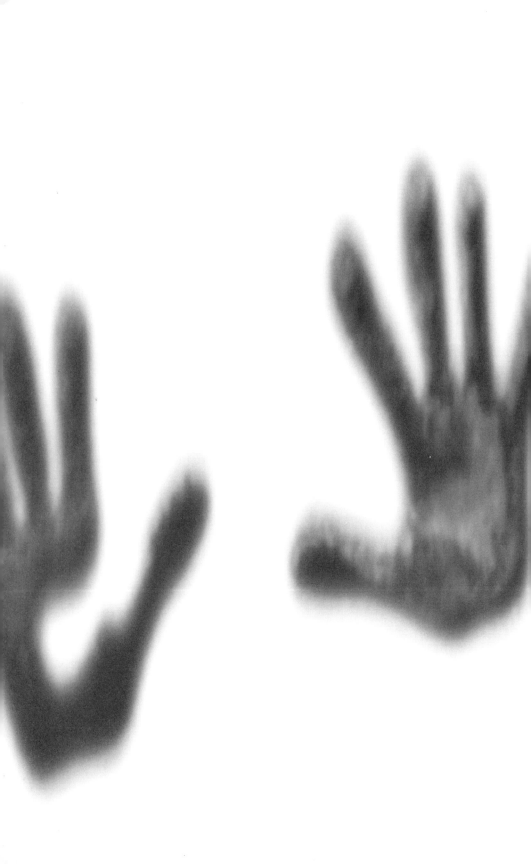

He who
does not fill his
world with
phantoms remains
alone.

antonio porchia

supernatural
superStars

Supernatural superstars have been sighted everywhere from Beverly Hills' chic Benedict Canyon to the lush hills of Hollywood. They run the gamut from celebrities who've seen ghosts to celebrities who've lived with ghosts to celebrities who are ghosts. One even fills the bill in all three categories.

✳

Bessie Love

the curse of vasquez

*G*hosts of murder victims often haunt the spot where the evil deed was done. Some of these souls are doomed to relive their untimely ends over and over. Some wish to leave survivors a clue about what really happened. Others grieve for a life cut short. The victims whose ghosts haunt Bessie Love's house were looking for something when they were killed, and death has not halted their search.

Above: Bessie Love was still a teenager when she entered films in 1915. **Left:** Scenic view in Bungalow Land in Laurel Canyon where ghosts of the Old West still roam.

Like her legendary contemporaries Lillian Gish and Mary Pickford, Bessie Love possessed the fragile, angelic beauty so characteristic of film stars of the 1910s. Under the direction of such pioneer filmmakers as D.W. Griffith and Thomas Ince, a teenage Bessie lit up the screen, and she established herself as a leading player of the silent era. Later, she made the transition to sound, where her singing and dancing in one of Hollywood's first musicals, 1929's *The Broadway Melody*, earned her an Academy Award nomination for Best Actress. In the mid '30s, Bessie moved to London, and there she continued her career on stage, screen, television and radio well into her eighties.

During a visit to Los Angeles in 1976, Bessie showed coauthor Marc Wanamaker the first home she ever owned—a Laurel Canyon abode she sold because she felt it was haunted.

Rustic Laurel Canyon is an area that has always attracted famous residents. At one time or another, such luminaries as John Gilbert, Roscoe "Fatty" Arbuckle, Tom Mix, Ramon Novarro, Charlie Chaplin, Frank Zappa, Jim Morrison, Joni Mitchell and California's ex-governor Jerry Brown have lived there.

As Marc and Bessie negotiated the steep two miles to the top of the canyon, she recalled earlier days, when the secluded rolling hills with sweeping views of the city were divided into a series of lots collectively known as Bungalow Land. In 1918, Bessie bought a one-bedroom cabin set back from the road on Lookout Mountain Drive.

Above: Leading lady of the silent screen, Bessie enthusiastically painted her first home.

She and other affluent folk from the movie industry moved to the canyon to enjoy a country lifestyle while still staying close to town. Walkways connected all the Bungalow Land cabins, leading through gardens up and down the hillside. Parties often erupted spontaneously in the village atmosphere, and Bessie remembered the great fun she had "bungalow-hopping" and greeting unexpected guests.

"Just after I bought the house," she told Marc, "I was warned about some curse on the property." She recounted the legend of Tiburcio Vasquez, a Mexican Robin Hood of the mid-1800s. For more than twenty years, Vasquez robbed from those newly-arrived citizens of California who had taken land from Mexican ranchers. Vasquez and his gang used the hidden trails and caves of the canyons that they knew so well to conceal their loot. As rumors of Vasquez's riches grew, others began searching in the hills for the buried treasure. Two such fortune hunters were unlucky enough to be caught on the very ground where Bessie's bungalow was to be built more than fifty years later. Vasquez killed them where they stood and cursed their spirits. Their ghosts were said to haunt the spot, constantly searching for Vasquez's ill-gotten gold.

Above: A postcard of "a shady nook in Laurel Canyon".

Bessie, barely twenty and not a believer in ghosts, enthusiastically moved into her first home. After settling in, she slowly became aware of odd happenings. Sometimes, she would hear a low, moaning sound. Doors would open and close by themselves. There were mysterious electrical problems. She tried to explain away the incidents at first, but over the next few years found them difficult to ignore. The doors and lights continued to operate of their own volition, but now she heard men's voices, too. And there were cold spots in the living room. She mentioned this to no one. . .until one spring evening in 1923.

While a girlfriend spent the night in a makeshift bed on the living room sofa, Bessie slept soundly in the bedroom. Bessie was awakened by the screams of her friend, who quickly burst through the door, terrified. "A ghost!" she cried. "I've just seen a ghost in your living room!" She dragged an apprehensive Bessie to the doorway. The young women peeked cautiously into the living room and were relieved to find it empty. "But I saw him," Bessie's friend insisted.

The sleeping guest had been awakened by the sound of a man's voice. She raised her head and quickly looked around the small room, which was well lit by a bright moon. No one was there. Then she heard the voice again and looked in the direction of the noise. Suddenly, the transparent figure of a man walked through the wall into the living room. He stood for a moment, adjusting his hat—a cowboy hat or sombrero. The young woman gasped, but the ghost seemed not to see her as he walked past the sofa toward the kitchen. That's when she leaped off the couch and ran to the bedroom, where the two women spent the remainder of the night huddled together.

Facing Page Inset: Bessie's bungalow today—a second bedroom and garage have been added.

Bessie never saw the ghost, nor did she have any desire to do so. Nonbeliever or not, she'd already seen and heard enough "funny stuff" during her five years in the bunga- low. After hearing her friend's story, Bessie packed her bags and moved out.

In late 1993, a twenty-nine-year-old film electrician named Bob Codik moved into the place. Some remodeling had begun nearly a decade earlier but never was completed, and the house had remained empty. On the hot, still days during the week they moved in, Codik and his roommate left the cabin door open. It was heavy, with an ancient lock that required just the right touch to get it to turn over in either direction. Twice that week, while the men were outside, the door quietly closed. They could explain that away. . .a gust of wind, although they'd felt none. But the door also locked. The second time, the deadbolt locked, too. Something was try- ing to keep them out. Having spent so much time on the property alone, the spirits were apparently reluctant to have guests.

Since then, Codik has experienced inexplicable electrical problems and a cold spot in the living room. Once, his was the only house in the area without power; his fully-charged cellular phone would not work until he drove blocks from the bungalow. Yet he has felt no further resis- tance to his presence in the house. More than a hundred years later, the curse of Vasquez endures as the ghosts of his victims continue to roam the canyon in search of lost treasure.

✳

Sharon Tate
and Paul Bern
unlikely bedfellows

*T*here are events so dramatic—and traumatic—in their effect on our lives that we often receive some kind of advance warning or vision. If we're lucky, we pay attention; we change a flight, take a different route home, don't let Tommy go swimming. It was actress Sharon Tate's cruel destiny to fall victim to one of the most savage slayings in Hollywood history. Three years before the actress and four others were brutally murdered by members of the Charles Manson "family" in 1969, Sharon saw a horrible specter of the bloody fate that awaited her. It was only one episode on a night full of ghostly goings-on in what was, undoubtedly, the second most terrifying night of her brief life.

Left: A Texas beauty queen and the future Mrs. Roman Polanski, Sharon Tate's grisly end at the hands of the Manson family was foreshadowed during a night of terror at the former home of Jean Harlow.

Sharon was twenty when she met twenty-nine-year-old Jay Sebring. Soon to be known as the premier men's hair stylist in Los Angeles, his client list would eventually include Paul Newman, Steve McQueen, Frank Sinatra, Sammy Davis Jr. and Henry Fonda. But in 1963, both Tate and Sebring were still struggling to make names for themselves.

The two dated for three years and even announced their engagement, but Sharon broke things off in 1966, when she met her future husband, director Roman Polanski. Jay was never bitter about the end of their romance. In fact, he came to look upon Sharon and Roman as his only real family. In 1969, with Sharon almost nine months pregnant and Roman on location with *The Day of the Dolphin* (a film he would not complete), it was Jay who kept her company at her home on Cielo Drive in Beverly Hills' posh Benedict Canyon—and Jay who died trying to protect her.

Top: Reporters gather at the Easton Drive home as the news of Bern's suicide spreads. **Inset:** Hairstylist to the stars, Jay Sebring bought the Harlow-Bern house because of its notorious history.

Jay also lived in Benedict Canyon, on nearby Easton Drive. He loved his Bavarian-style home, particularly the gutter spouts — life-size, hand-carved wooden likenesses of silent-screen stars like Pickford, Fairbanks and Valentino. But some people claimed the house was jinxed. It had once been the unhappy home of Jean Harlow, the screen's first platinum bombshell, and her husband, MGM producer Paul Bern, who shot himself there in 1932. Later, two others drowned in the swimming pool. But Jay didn't believe in jinxes. Perhaps he should have.

One night in 1966, Sharon stayed in the Easton Drive house alone. Almost immediately, she felt weird; "funny" was all she could say to reporter Dick Kleiner, who later wrote about the experience. Unable to explain why, Sharon was frightened by every little noise and lay awake in Jay's bed with the lights on. Suddenly, "a creepy little man" came into the bedroom. She felt sure it was Paul Bern. The man ignored Sharon as he skulked about the room, apparently looking for something. Sharon threw on her robe and hurried out.

What she told Kleiner next chilled him to the bone. Halfway down the stairs, she gasped, stunned at what she saw. Tied to the posts was a figure—she could not tell if it was a man or woman. But she could clearly see that the person's throat had been cut.

Sharon ran to the living room to pour herself a drink but couldn't find where Jay kept the liquor. She felt a strong urge to press on one of the

Inset: A 21-year-old Jean Harlow at her wedding to 42-year-Paul Bern, July 1932.

bookcases; it suddenly opened to reveal a hidden bar. Shivering with fright, she filled a glass, sat down and tried to steady her nerves.

Another urge took hold, and she tore away wallpaper at the base of the bar, uncovering a solid copper base.

Confused, she finished her drink and headed back toward the bedroom. The ghastly apparition was still visible on the stairs, but the man had left the bedroom and was now lurking in the upstairs hallway. She made it to the bed and, remarkably, fell instantly asleep.

In the morning, Sharon thought it had all been some terrible nightmare, a dream . . . until she saw the wallpaper she had torn away from the bar. She had indeed seen Paul Bern and, unknowingly, had glimpsed her own terrible fate. One can only wonder if Jay also became disturbed by things he saw in the house. Maybe that's why he was at Sharon's house that deadly night in 1969.

✳

Top: Mild-mannered Bern in 1927 at Paramount. **Top Right:** Bern's master bedroom where Tate saw his ghost. **Bottom Right:** The stairs where Tate saw a horrible foreshadowing of her own death.

Grace Moore, Clifton Webb and Mom *together again*

*T*he stucco house north of Sunset Boulevard on Rexford Drive was the kind of place Hollywood stars lived in once they'd made it to the top. Set back from the street, it had a Spanish influence, with a side and back wing forming a central courtyard. In the heart of Beverly Hills, it was home to many celebrities over the years, the frequent setting for lavish parties . . . and for ghosts.

The house was built in 1921 by silent-screen director Arthur Rosson, whose wife, Lucille, got the house when the couple divorced. She went on to marry director Victor Fleming of *The Wizard of Oz* and *Gone With the Wind* fame. They later leased out the house to such stellar tenants as Marlene Dietrich and Metropolitan Opera soprano Grace Moore.

Left: The Ghost of Rexford Drive, Clifton Webb in the 1954 romantic hit *Three Coins in a Fountain.*

Grace, a vivacious blonde, had also starred on Broadway before MGM lured her to Hollywood in 1930, but the studio canceled her contract after only two films. Undaunted, she signed with Columbia and starred in a string of successful musicals that helped to popularize opera and made her famous. She loved to entertain on Rexford Drive, often hosting lively parties where she would dance the night away.

In 1943 the Flemings sold the house to actors Gene and Kathleen Lockhart, who also liked to receive guests there. A frequent visitor was their good friend Clifton Webb. Clifton adored the house and regularly asked if he could buy it, but Gene refused to sell until daughter June (the future mom on Lassie) finished high school. Finally, in 1947, Gene agreed. Clifton immediately wrote a check.

Above: Grace Moore was nominated for "Best Actress" in 1934 for *One Night of Love.* Clifton Webb saw her ghost in his house. **Upper Right:** Supporting player in more than a hundred films, Gene Lockhart sold the Rexford Drive house to Webb.

Clifton Webb was already a seasoned performer by the age of ten. In his teens, he made his mark both as a leading ballroom dancer and as a singer with the Boston Opera. He appeared in a smattering of silent films but found true stardom on the stage. In London and on Broadway, he enjoyed friendships with Noel Coward, Marilyn Miller, Jeanne Eagels, Grace Moore and a young Humphrey Bogart. In 1944, at age fifty-three, he returned to the screen in *Laura* and received an Oscar nomination for Best Supporting Actor. He was nominated again in 1946 for his performance in *The Razor's Edge*.

The fastidious Clifton was at the height of his career when he moved into the Rexford Drive house along with his mother, Maybelle. When his dear friend Noel Coward came west, Clifton even added a guest room, which he dubbed "the Greek room." He loved to fill the place with people, and his parties became famous for their mixture of stage and screen luminaries.

During Clifton's first year on Rexford Drive, Grace Moore was killed in a plane crash in Europe. As time passed, Webb confided to friend and psychic Kenny Kingston that he'd seen her ghost more than once in the house. When Maybelle died in 1959, Clifton retired and became a recluse, keeping all of her belongings in a locked room. Several days before he died in October of 1966, he told Kingston, "I'm not leaving this house — even at death."

In 1967, producer Douglas Cramer and his wife, Joyce Haber, the gossip columnist who replaced the late Hedda Hopper at the Los Angeles Times, purchased the house. During the Cramers' first night in the house, Doug's mother stayed in the Greek room. According to ghost hunter Hans Holzer, she had placed her toothbrush on the sink in the adjoining bathroom but did not find it there the next morning. Instead, she saw it protruding from a hidden wall receptacle that had not been exposed the night before. Confused, she tried to leave the bathroom, but the door suddenly jammed. Nearly hysterical, she had to climb out the window.

Two months later, following the birth of his son, Doug's half-sister paid her first visit to the house. She had recently quit smoking, but on her first morning in the Greek room she found a squashed pack of cigarettes on the sink. A week later, she woke to find more cigarettes, all crushed and broken and strewn across the bedroom. Once, she felt herself being hugged by a warm but invisible presence in her bed. The toilet paper in the bathroom would often unroll by itself, and twice, she woke in the morning to find that the toilet had been used and not flushed — though no one had been in there all night.

Several times, while sitting by the pool, both Doug and Joyce saw a swaying figure in the master bedroom. "It was a dark, transparent shadow the size and shape of Clifton," recalls Doug. "I never saw it up close, as Joyce did. I only saw it through a window when I was outside. I didn't see clothes or details, but it always resembled Clifton and seemed ageless."

Facing Page: The ghost of Rexford Drive, Clifton Webb as Mr. Belvedere in one of his biggest hits, *Sitting Pretty*, 1948.

Doug also saw shadows the size and shape of Maybelle in the hallway. As if to confirm his sightings, the dogs began to react to cold spots in the hallway between the guest bedroom and the den—an area Clifton had often paced during bouts of insomnia. "They wouldn't go near the cold spots without barking and often urinating on the spot," Doug says.

The maid and butler told Holzer that lights would go on and off by themselves; the two had also seen the figure of a man. On a hunch, Joyce brought home one of Clifton's films. "Not only did the servants identify him," said Kingston, "but when the dogs saw his image on the screen, all three began howling."

One October evening, nothing could quiet one of the dogs. He howled all night, and Joyce heard disturbing moans in the bedroom. When she investigated, she saw a gray figure in the corner. As she later discovered, that night happened to be the first anniversary of Clifton's death. Another night, she was awakened by the rustling of the bedroom curtains. A dark form moved back and forth across the room, and a voice said, "Well, well . . . " Clifton's friends confirmed that he was in the habit of sighing those words. Joyce saw and heard this for several days. Then she began receiving telepathic impressions telling her that Clifton wanted them to stay.

And stay they did. At the time, the Cramers were considered one of Hollywood's hottest couples; Joyce wielded tremendous power with her column, while Doug reaped huge profits from producing such shows as *Love, American Style*, *The Brady Bunch* and *The Odd Couple*. (He would later produce *The Love Boat* and *Dynasty*.) The couple carried on the home's long tradition of extravagant entertaining. On any given night, the guest list for a party or private screening might include Lucille Ball, Fred Astaire, Truman Capote, Henry Kissinger, Gore Vidal or Mae West, who was godmother to the Cramers' daughter.

There was rarely any ghostly activity during the Cramer soirees, but Joyce continued to see Clifton in the living room, and once, quite clearly, in the courtyard just outside her bedroom window. He was looking directly at her. Then he vanished.

Disturbed by Clifton's presence, Joyce asked Holzer to hold a seance. On a Thursday night in October of 1968, he arrived at the house accompanied by famed psychic Sybil Leek, who had been told nothing of the house or even why she was there. Also present were playwright Garson Kanin and his wife, spirited actress Ruth Gordon—both friends of Webb. "The seance convinced everyone that Clifton was in the house," Doug confirms. "And the medium, Sybil, did become Clifton in mood and spirit and intent—and most particularly in language and dialect. She mentioned things that only those who knew Clifton well could possibly know, things that Sybil or Hans could never have known."

Although the seance finally convinced Doug to take Clifton's presence seriously, the problem had solved itself. After that night, Clifton was never seen in the house again. Nor was Maybelle. The dogs even stopped barking in the hallway.

The Cramers divorced in 1972, and Joyce sold the house a few years later. (She died in 1993.) Subsequent owners reported apparitions of a man and woman dancing in the entry hall. They believed the man was Clifton but were unclear whether the shadowy figure of the woman was Maybelle or Grace. Whoever they were, the last waltz ended for the dancers a few years ago. The Rexford Drive house, scene of so much gaiety and glamour, was torn down and replaced by a more modern residence. And since it was the house, not the land, that Clifton, Maybelle and Grace loved so much, their spirits have disappeared along with it.

✳

Ozzie Nelson

won't give up the ghost

*B*andleader and star of radio and television, Ozzie Nelson was such a health enthusiast that when he was diagnosed with cancer of the liver at age sixty-eight, it came as a shock both to him and his family. It seemed so unfair; he lived right, ate well, never smoked. He was not ready to leave his wife, his children and grandchildren. Nor was he ready to leave the lovely home where he'd spent his happiest years. Many believe he may still inhabit that famous house—something does.

Facing Page: Amorous Ozzie Nelson and his lovely Harriet, 1951. **Above:** Ozzie and Harriet instruct sons Ricky and David in the art of television makeup.

For more than twenty-five years, Ozzie and Harriet Nelson lived in a handsome, two-story colonial home on Camino Palmero Drive at the base of the Hollywood Hills. Their boys, David and Ricky, spent their teenage years there. The gracious residence fit the family's screen image so well that the Nelsons used it as a model for their set in *The Adventures of Ozzie and Harriet* and occasionally used it for exterior shots. Harriet stayed on after Ozzie's death in 1975, but sold the house five years later.

The new owners were soon frightened by baffling events: footsteps in the night, faucets and lights turning on and off by themselves, doors suddenly opening and closing. They asked parapsychologist Dr. Barry Taff to investigate.

Above: The Nelson home, where Ozzie may still walk the halls.

Taff questioned the people about the noises but felt they were holding something back. "This is very difficult to talk about," the woman finally relented. Something—or someone—unseen was "getting fresh" with her. At night while she was asleep, her covers would be pulled back, and she would feel someone kissing her neck and breasts. Each time, when she woke up, the covers were down, but no one was there.

Taff assured her that this was by no means uncommon: "There are many reports of sexual activity with regard to ghosts." He mentioned a similar problem actress Susan Strasberg had in 1966 with a ghost pulling down her bedcovers. Men and women alike, he said, have reported being undressed and caressed by unseen hands. This did not comfort the owners. Frazzled and upset, they ended the investigation and moved out. But it seems the ghost stayed.

In June of 1994, a lone painter, who had been hearing footsteps in the empty house for weeks, was frightened by the sudden appearance of a milky white form next to him. He couldn't tell if it was Ozzie; there were no distinct features. During those few seconds, the only thing he could make out clearly was a foot, but he unquestionably felt a presence. Looks like Ozzie has disproved Thomas Wolfe; you *can* go home again.

✳

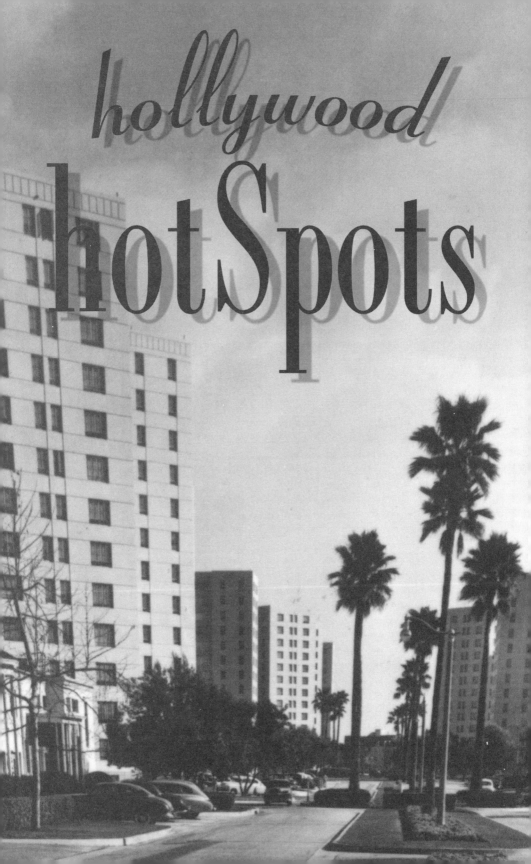

hollywood
hotSpots

Hot Spots encompasses a wide variety of locales, from the lush, wooded canyon of Beverly Glen to the famous intersection of Hollywood and Vine. Here, we follow a long stretch of history and an array of spirits that includes Native Americans, the Mob, Bela Lugosi and a man who literally lost his head over a woman.

*

Hollywood and Vine

the final bow

*T*he world-famous corner of Hollywood and Vine is a mere ghost of the busy, sophisticated intersection it once was. For forty years, a stone's throw from Hollywood's top theaters, restaurants, radio stations and movie studios, Hollywood and Vine was one sure place to see a star. The Brown Derby, NBC, The Palace, Hollywood Legion Stadium, RKO, Paramount, Earl Carroll's—eager fans and autograph hounds could plant themselves outside any of these establishments to catch a glimpse of their favorite celebrities.

Facing Page: Bob Cummings and Marsha Hunt pose for publicity shots in 1936. **Above:** Suave Bela Lugosi and one of his beloved cigars.

Famed horror-film star Bela Lugosi commanded this stretch of the Boulevard. As Dracula, he held audiences in the grip of terror, the embodiment of aristocratic evil. Bela was aristocratic in his private life as well, a cultured man of the Old World, proud and traditional. Such values helped provide order in the transitory world of acting. And so, whether Bela was on top of the world or struggling to pay his rent, he strolled along Hollywood Boulevard at Vine Street every day.

"He loved Hollywood, and walking that stretch was a ritual for him," says friend Marie Staats, receptionist for twenty-five years at Utter McKinley Mortuary on Hollywood Boulevard, a block east of Vine. Bela stopped in regularly to chat with Marie and her husband.

In 1959, Marie organized the hundreds of fans who lined the Boulevard outside Utter McKinley to pay their last respects to Bela as he lay in state, dressed in black tie and his Dracula cape. But it wasn't until Bela was on his way to the cemetery that he was ready for his final bow.

Above: Lugosi's favorite walk, with the William Strother Mortuary – later Utter McKinley– in lower left. **Facing page, upper left:** The bus bench where the ghost of Lon Chaney was seen for years after his death. **Facing page, inset:** The master of horror, Lon Chaney.

The mortuary had an agreement with the Hollywood Chamber of Commerce not to travel the Boulevard. The last thing thriving businesses wanted was a funeral procession going by. As usual, the driver of the hearse carrying Bela headed north, preparing to cross Hollywood Boulevard. "Suddenly," the driver later told Marie, "it was as if someone tugged at the wheel." Instead of crossing Hollywood, the hearse veered left and up the Boulevard. The driver struggled, but the coach had a mind of its own. He was unable to regain control of the wheel until they crossed Vine. "I don't know what happened . . . I just don't know," he told her, visibly shaken. But Marie knew, and she smiled. It was Bela saying goodbye to his beloved Hollywood Boulevard.

On Bela's last ride past Hollywood and Vine, he may have driven past another master of menace. The great Lon Chaney had been slated to star in *Dracula*, but he died before filming could begin. He reigned as the silent screen's *Man of a Thousand Faces*, with *The Hunchback of Notre Dame* and *The Phantom of the Opera* among his unforgettable portrayals. Like Bela, Lon also had a particular fondness for this intersection; after his death, his ghost was regularly spotted sitting on a bus bench at Hollywood and Vine. When the bench was removed, the sightings ceased. The ghost of Lon Chaney has not been seen there since, but you can still wait an eternity for a bus in Hollywood.

✳

The Holly Mont Haunting

a plethora of the paranormal

*P*arapsychologist *Barry Taff's most famous case was chronicled in the 1983 film* **The Entity**, *but his experiences at two Hollywood homes on Holly Mont Drive turned out to be his most extraordinary. There, he was able to document more sustained phenomena in a finite period than in any episode before or since.*

It all began in May 1976, when Dr. Taff was a research associate in UCLA's Neuropsychiatric Institute. An undergraduate burst into the lab, excited about events he'd witnessed the night before at a party in the Hollywood Hills: Objects flew around the room, and mysterious shadows appeared in his peripheral view. A female guest was pinned to the wall by a chair that suddenly zoomed across the room in full sight of the guests. An instant later, a kettle soared from the stove into the living room and dumped water over the helpless woman. Later, the houseboy was chased through the home by a cabbage with a huge butcher knife lodged in its side; he quit on the spot.

Facing Page: Statue near the tunnels found by Dexter Grey, connecting the homes and leading to the grave of a woman.

Taff's curiosity went into overdrive. Ninety percent of his cases meet the criteria for poltergeist activity: flying or mysteriously disappearing objects, slamming doors. But this has nothing to do with ghosts. Poltergeist activity, he explains, "is now theorized to stem directly from the presence of pubescent and/or adolescent children in a rather tense, conflict-ridden, emotionally chaotic environment." As in the 1976 film *Carrie*, the child becomes a psychokinetic agent, unconsciously unleashing pandemonium and mayhem.

However, that still leaves a number of cases that do suggest the presence of what Taff calls "discarnate intelligence"—a disembodied consciousness. And the description of events at the party had all the earmarks of it.

Taff was delighted to be invited to another party at the house that very night. "Never in my wildest dreams," he says, "did I ever imagine that

Above and Facing Page: Jolly's house on the left and Grey's on the right—two of the most haunted homes in the Hollywood hills.

this would turn into one of the most incredible cases in our files suggesting discarnate intelligence."

The beautiful Spanish house was built in 1924 on a narrow road called Holly Mont, near the base of Beachwood Canyon. In 1976, the occupant was Don Jolly, a round, mustachioed man in his late thirties. He invited Taff into the grand two-story foyer, lit by an elaborate wrought-iron chandelier, then into the living room, with its magnificent view of Los Angeles. Jolly explained that the activity had escalated over his seven years in the house to its present chaos. He confided that he was now terrified and planned to move out. "I hope something happens so you can see what I mean."

Taff didn't have to wait long. As the two talked, several books began to fly across the room. A telephone lifted off a stand and sailed over Jolly's shoulder, barely missing Taff, who also dodged a large glass jar.

Then the doorbell began ringing relentlessly, Taff remembers, "as if some madman was outside seeking entrance." He examined the wiring and was shocked to discover it was rotted through—the doorbell was completely disconnected. When Taff asked permission to investigate further, Jolly consented.

Ten days later, Taff and a film crew from a local TV station assembled in the dining room. Suddenly, an ice tray came spiraling out of the kitchen and crashed against the far wall of the dining room. Then a large sack of cloth napkins soared through the air, striking a silver platter directly in front of reporter Connie Fox. Next, a pewter goblet sailed across the room into the wall.

That was only the beginning. A massive world atlas abruptly appeared, its pages open and flapping like a bird. It chased the terrified Fox, who ran screaming, but the book stayed on her tail. Even when she bolted down the front Z-shaped stairway, the book followed, making three ninety-degree turns. "When one of my friends laughed about it," Taff recalls, "an old shoe flew around the outside of the house and struck him in the head." Whatever it was that caused these disturbances, it seemed to pick its targets. Taff was convinced this "thing" was intelligent.

Taff and Jolly moved to a storage area between the dining room and the kitchen. Suddenly, coins—primarily pennies and dimes—began to fall from the ceiling. "Thousands of coins pelted us," Taff says. "They appeared to fall from thin air."

And still there was more. A large black robe wrapped itself around the wrought-iron chandelier. "One instant the chandelier was empty," Taff says, "and the next second, the robe appeared, intricately wrapped around the workings of the fixture. It required several minutes on a stepladder to remove it."

Meanwhile, whenever the news crew tried to use electrical outlets in the house, the power to those particular lines was cut off; other lines remained unaffected. Taff checked the fuse box; there was no evidence of tampering. "Whatever force was accomplishing this feat, it could selectively negate the power along specific circuits. Even the crew's battery-powered equipment refused to function in the house." The street lamp directly in front of the house also blinked erratically, but the rest of the block's lights were undisturbed.

Jolly asked a local bishop to bless the house; when he arrived, his hat immediately apported from the top of his head to an inaccessible part of the roof. (To apport is to disappear and reappear with no visible means of transport.) When the bishop attempted to use his holy water scepter, the top exploded off its base.

For the remainder of the evening, Taff, Jolly and the others continued to see and hear amazing things: A large shower head from the master bath came flying down the stairs into the living room, managing to miss all fifteen people in the room; several sharp, explosive sounds came from the hallway; coasters from the dining table took off and traveled to the living room; several chairs in the dining room changed locations; a thick chain and padlock appeared around the front door and gate, locking everyone in; a fire broke out in a bathroom waste-basket.

The news report attracted both local and national attention, and Jolly had had enough. He packed up and moved out. But Taff wasn't frightened; he admits being occasionally shocked, but never scared. He wanted to see more.

Taff stayed in the house for the next nine days, witnessing dozens of unexplainable events. He saw the stove turn itself on and pull away from the wall. Doors locked, bolted and unlocked by themselves. Once, he put a glass of iced tea on the kitchen counter. When he turned back, it was gone; he later found it behind a door he'd locked the previous evening.

Close to midnight on Taff's fourth night in the house, he heard something approach the master bedroom. It grabbed the doorknob, jiggled it and turned it to the right. Taff opened the door but found nothing.

Though he was alone in the house, footsteps in the kitchen woke him up almost three hours later. Some six hours after that, as he sat on the living room couch, he heard "the sounds and sensations of someone walking down the stairway and up behind me. I distinctly smelled a strong, sweet perfume, but I didn't see anyone."

Taff continued to hear footsteps throughout the house. One evening, he observed "a dark, humanoid form" in the dining room but was unable to distinguish any specific characteristics or gender.

During his stay, Taff met concert pianist Dexter Grey, Jolly's neighbor, and was surprised that he, too, was experiencing paranormal activity. He'd heard voices and footsteps and had seen the apparition of a woman. He invited Taff to see for himself. During the investigation, they witnessed lights flickering, furniture moving and a chandelier swinging violently. Grey's friend, photographer Joseph Jasgur, vividly recalls the swinging chandelier, as well as another peculiar phenomenon: "Sometimes, when Dexter played the piano, organ music came out of the walls."

Grey showed Taff the house's most startling feature—a secret passageway behind a built-in bookshelf he'd discovered during remodeling. It connected to a series of subterranean tunnels linking several houses on the hillside. Grey suspected the tunnels led to a monastery, but Taff believed they dated to the Prohibition era and had been used for storing and moving bootleg liquor.

Still, the passageways were only part of the story. While exploring the tunnel beneath his house, Grey found a makeshift grave. The headstone read "Regina 1922." Could Regina be the female apparition seen and smelled throughout both houses? Was she killed and secretly buried in the passageway? Would bootleggers stop to make a headstone? Why would monks have concealed a dead body? Was her grave here first, before the house? Unfortunately, since Grey did not wish to disturb the remains, no further information could be obtained.

Taff was sorry to have to leave such an active site just when he and the "presence" were getting used to each other. As both began to relax, the activity increased. "We tried to anger it, tried everything under the sun. It just did whatever it wanted, whenever it wanted to do it."

Before new tenants moved in, Taff left a note on UCLA stationery offering further assistance. He taped it inside a kitchen cupboard. Several weeks later, he received a call from a woman who lived several miles from the Holly Mont house. She was perplexed by a note—Taff's note—she found stuck inside her closet. "She had absolutely no relationship to the new owners," Taff marvels. "I've heard of apports, but this is ridiculous!"

✳

I Love Roxbury!

lucille ball's home sweet home

The First Lady *of television, Lucille Ball, was very attached to the house at 1000 North Roxbury Drive. Over the course of more than thirty years there, she raised her children, divorced one husband and married another. Her neighbors were two of her oldest and dearest friends in Hollywood: Jack Benny to the north and Jimmy Stewart to the south. Pals Rosie Clooney and Esther Williams were just up the street. All had been to parties in her home. The second half of her life unfolded on Roxbury Drive. Only death ended her reign there. Or did it?*

PROPERTY OF MECHANICS' INSTITUTE

Facing Page: The Queen of RKO grew up to own the studio and became a tough boss who demanded complete control. **Above:** The house was not on the market when Lucy talked the owners into selling it to her in 1954.

In 1954, Desilu Studios had reached its peak. It could continue at that level or try to compete with the big boys: MGM, Paramount, Universal. *I Love Lucy* was number one and would provide an income for Lucy and Desi for the rest of their lives. Desi suggested that they quit the show and work when they chose. He would run the studio as it was and Lucy could be at home in their beloved Chatsworth *ranchito*. Without missing a beat, Lucy chose to continue with the show. From that moment, the marriage was doomed.

Once she made the decision to continue working, Lucy began the search for a new home. She decided to look in exclusive Beverly Hills. She took pleasure in having made it to Beverly Hills, having the status to move into what was at that time the ultimate neighborhood. A broker showed her a house at 1001 North Roxbury Drive, but Lucy took a liking to the house across the street. "It's not on the market," the broker said. "We'll see about that," said Lucy. She left the stunned broker at the curb and knocked on the front door.

Mrs. Bang answered. Lucy made an offer of seventy-five thousand dollars. Mr. Bang raised it to eighty-five thousand dollars. They shook on it. Lucy returned to the broker and said she had bought the house.

One of the first to welcome the family was next-door-neighbor Jack Benny. Early one morning, the kitchen door flew open and in walked Benny, playing his violin. He walked around the breakfast table, playing passionately all the while, walked out the door and left. It was the ultimate neighborhood, all right. Tour buses with ogling fans cruised by, stopping in front of her house and those of her famous neighbors.

Above: For Lucy and Desi, this was a house, but never a home. The couple divorced five years after moving here.

Desi spent a relatively small amount of time at home, shuttling back and forth between studio lots. As far as he was concerned, the home on Roxbury Drive was never home. Their personal life was spinning out of control and Lucy couldn't save it. The final straw came in 1959 when Lucy found Desi in bed with two ladies of the night. They divorced in 1960.

In the fall of 1961, Lucy married comedian Gary Morton. He loved the house and enjoyed planning improvements with his bride. Lucy held court in the downstairs den. This was her arena, with a white carpet. A world-class backgammon and Scrabble player, she had a custom-made backgammon table. Nearby was a master panel from which she controlled the lighting, temperature and the Frank Sinatra records playing in the background. The den was filled with the laughter of guests such as George Burns, Jack Benny, Bob Hope, Milton Berle, Kaye Ballard, Jimmy Stewart, Hank Fonda, Ginger Rogers and many more.

The house on Roxbury remained Lucy's home until her death in April of 1989. Several years later, Morton sold the property. The new owners tore down the neighborhood landmark. Fans gathered at the construction site to mourn the end of an era.

Fans were not the only ones who were sad to see the place go. A friend of Lucy's drove by one sunny afternoon and pulled over to look at the destruction. Walls were missing and he could see into Lucy's bedroom and her fabled den. He noticed a woman walking around the perimeter of the property, peering through the fence at what was left of the home. The woman was tall, thin, a redhead. She turned toward him for a moment and he held his breath. It was Lucy. "She looked upset and a little confused," said the friend. Lucy liked to be in control and clearly she no longer was. "It was upsetting for her. I sensed frustration and a deep melancholy. She walked around the south corner of the house and disappeared."

The friend had never seen a ghost before—or since. He fears ridicule and prefers to remain anonymous. But he is quite sure of what he saw that day. How ironic that his last encounter with the world's funniest lady filled him with sadness.

*

The Nelsons' Mulholland House

rick, tracy and shades of errol flynn

*T*een idol-turned-pop legend Rick Nelson loved living in Errol Flynn's home. Flynn, the swashbuckling superstar, had some high times in the Hollywood Hills with lots of wine, women and song. No slouch in that department either, Nelson felt a strong kinship with the spirit of Flynn. Perhaps Flynn felt it, too. His spirit—or someone else's—may have tried to warn Rick of the tragic fate that lay ahead of him.

Facing Page: Rick and Chris Nelson's clean-scrubbed looks belied their troubled lives. The Mulholland house had been the scene of some of Hollywood's wildest parties, but the Nelsons knew only unhappiness there. **Above:** "I designed the house myself," Errol Flynn wrote in his autobiography, *My Wicked, Wicked Ways.* "I would make of it a playhouse."

"…All the heroes in one magnificent, sexy, animal package" is how Jack Warner characterized Errol Flynn. A scoundrel with an irresistible twinkle in his eye, Flynn was what every woman wanted and what every man wanted to be. To celebrate his good fortune in filmland, Flynn designed his dream house—he called it his "playhouse." His dream was fulfilled in 1941 when he bought eleven and a half acres in the Hollywood Hills off Mulholland Drive and built a sprawling farm-house. An unbroken line of windows provided a panoramic view of the city below. Flynn also included an elaborate bar, several mysterious secret passageways, and more than a few peepholes. Outside, he built a black-bottomed pool and circular stables that he copied from the Lippizaner stables in Vienna.

For many years, Flynn lived the good life at his Mulholland home. In 1957, not yet divorced from third wife Patrice Wymore, the forty-eight-year-old Flynn took up with fifteen-year-old Beverly Aadland. Beverly's mother, Florence, went along for the ride as often as possible, and the two women spent many nights in the home. But by then, Errol's "wicked, wicked ways" had taken an enormous toll. Bloated and in ill health, he finally lost the home he loved so much in 1959 to his first wife, Lili Damita, whose alimony was long overdue. He died later that same year.

In 1959, nineteen-year-old Ricky Nelson was driving teenage girls crazy on both the big and small screen. He'd joined his parents and his brother David on radio's *The Adventures of Ozzie and Harriet* at age four. The show moved to television in 1952 and ran fourteen years. During that time, the world watched Ricky transform from irksome preteen to rock music idol. Eventually he married and had his own family. In 1977, he found the perfect home for them. He bought the Flynn estate from country and western artist Stuart Hamblin, its only other owner. Rick and his wife, actress Chris Nelson, moved into the home with their four children just eighteen years after Flynn's demise.

"The house was a two-story ranch house. It wasn't oversized or grandiose in any way, but it was sprawling," daughter Tracy said. "The front door was in a place where it shouldn't have been, so we never used it. Because of that I never really felt that the house had a heart; it had no

center. I would usually just come in and
go straight up to my room."

"My bedroom used to be Beverly
Aadland's, and we used to smell this
funky, cheap perfume. All sorts of weird
things went on: my shower door would
open and close in the middle of the night;
the toilet would flush; my shades would
roll up for no reason." The ghost in her
room felt distinctly feminine. Ms.
Aadland is still living. Could it have
been her mother? Instinctively, Tracy felt
it was an older presence. "This is going
to sound so crazy, but it didn't feel like a
young, naïve girl. It felt like a cynical
presence." A cynical woman in Flynn's
house? That could have been any number of women Flynn had loved
and "forfeited." Whoever or whatever was there, Tracy's friends felt it
too. "When I was going to school, girls would have slumber parties, but
nobody would stay at my house. To me it was like having a pet, 'Oh
well, it's just that weird energy in the house.'"

Rick and Chris Nelson's home life was nothing like the happy family we
saw on *The Adventures of Ozzie and Harriet*. The couple was plagued by
problems—with their marriage, their careers and with drugs. In the
early eighties, Chris moved out with their twin boys. The youngest son
went to live with Chris' mother. Tracy remained with her dad.

"I was doing *Square Pegs* at the time," Tracy remembers. "One night, I
arrived home from work. It was dark. I looked up at the dining room and
the light was on. There was a man standing in the dining room. I thought,
'Oh, Pop's home.' I went upstairs and called to him—no answer. His car
was gone and there was nobody there. Then the phone rang and it was
Pop calling from the road to say he'd be home tomorrow."

Left: Dashing, romantic and adventurous, Errol Flynn became one of the most popular stars in
the world.

Tracy told him what she had just seen and Rick replied, "Oh that's just Errol."

The following day, Tracy came home from work while it was still daylight. She went straight to her room to read. After a few minutes, there was a noise from downstairs. It sounded like someone had broken in.

"My father had a room below mine full of his gold records and awards, all hanging on the walls. It sounded like whoever was down there was smashing Dad's gold records. I remember thinking, 'Oh my God, take anything, but don't take those.'"

"I hid myself in the closet and I waited for the noise to stop. It was really loud, the house was shaking. It sounded like people were throwing things against the walls, breaking chairs and breaking glass. The sun finally went down. It had been quiet for a while and I thought it was safe to go downstairs."

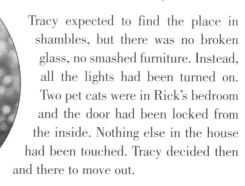

Tracy expected to find the place in shambles, but there was no broken glass, no smashed furniture. Instead, all the lights had been turned on. Two pet cats were in Rick's bedroom and the door had been locked from the inside. Nothing else in the house had been touched. Tracy decided then and there to move out.

After she moved into her own apartment, Rick and his girlfriend phoned her one night. "The weirdest thing happened," they told her. "We were downstairs and we heard all this noise coming from your room. We thought we were being robbed. Things were crashing and breaking. We called the police, ran outside down the driveway and waited for them to come. When they got here," the couple continued, "the police went upstairs to investigate. Your door was locked from

---

Above: The spirit in Tracy Nelson's bedroom started out as playful, but after her father's tragic death, it turned deeply malevolent.

the inside." When they opened it, they discovered that all the lights in the room had been turned on, but not a thing had been touched.

Rick Nelson lived in the Mulholland house for two more years, until his death in a 1985 plane crash. Tracy recalls that the spirit in the house changed dramatically after his death. "It had been playful before, but after my father died, it turned malevolent. When he left, everything just turned ugly and scary in the house. My ex-husband always had a hard time believing any of this ghost stuff. After Dad died, we were removing some furniture and he went outside and refused to go back in. He told me, 'Something's in that house and I don't want to be anywhere near it.'"

The Mulholland house stood vacant after Rick Nelson's death. During that time, darkness seemed to completely envelop the place. A gang broke in and murdered a girl in the living room. Then a mysterious fire burned half the house. The ruins were torn down, the acreage divided into separate lots and sold.

"I've tried to figure it out. There was a lot of really wacky stuff going on in terms of drug usage in the house when I was growing up. I believe all that stuff creates energetic chaos—I don't know what else to call it. So it was a wacky place to live. Compound that with the history of the place."

"All the women on my mother's side are very psychic: my grandmother, my mom, me. Since I was a kid, I've always been very open to the possibility of ghosts because I always felt them. I never saw anything, but I felt them. All I can tell you is that the house was definitely haunted."

Tracy has a theory about the two explosive, smashing episodes. Perhaps Flynn or the cynical woman was trying to warn Rick of impending tragedy. When the warnings failed and Rick was killed at age forty-five—before his time, like Errol—the spirit turned black. "My father's death was such a cataclysmic thing for the family…maybe the smashing was a warning…who knows?"

✳

Castillo del Lago
madonna goes bugsy

*E*ven if people do not believe in ghosts, they might still be apprehensive about moving into a house with an eerie history. The tragic victims of the 1969 Manson murders may not have haunted the house on Cielo Drive, but few people wanted to live at the scene of such violence and evil. (The house was eventually torn down in 1994.) But a dubious past did not seem to bother Madonna, who was quite comfortable with one of her own. For four years, she lived in the extraordinary Castillo del Lago, a twenty-thousand-square-foot mansion towering nine stories above Beachwood Canyon. But the elegant home, once a playground for the denizens of the underworld, still housed some of the darker inhabitants from the nether world.

Facing Page: The Queen of Pop did not feel safe behind her castle walls. Was the ghost of Bugsy Siegel to blame? **Inset:** She festooned Castillo del Lago with stripes—which scared neighbors.

Completed in 1926, the massive home took three years to build. The living quarters compose the sixth and seventh floors. The lower levels are used for offices, servants' quarters, and storage. The upper floors open onto formal gardens, terraces with fountains and a swimming pool, all with magnificent views of Lake Hollywood to the west and the Hollywood sign to the east. Former owners Don and Alice Willfong believe that gangster Bugsy Siegel leased the hillside castle for elite, invitation-only parties during the thirties. Revelers were free to drink, gamble and listen to entertainers such as Ruth Etting, the pioneer radio and recording star who later married "Moe the Gimp" Snyder. Cautious by necessity, Siegel had his boys remove concrete steps that led to the street on both sides of the house to prevent unwanted visitors. The private driveway, which hid a series of dungeon-like rooms underneath, and the long stone tunnel leading to the elevator, deterred police interference. Despite all the precautions, local legend says a rival gang, or maybe even the Feds, successfully raided the place from a neighboring house and bumped off a few of Bugsy's gang. True or not, many visitors to the house feel a deep sense of foreboding. Just ask Tom Murray, a charming British fashion photographer who had a three-day shoot there in 1988.

"One of the actors who played Tarzan lived there for a while and was into black magic; that's what we heard. When we were shooting, there was a very weird girl living there and we were only allowed to be in half of the house," Murray recalls. "It really didn't matter because we all hated being inside so much. The models particularly disliked it. They were all freezing cold inside. We shot most of the film outside." Murray didn't have much choice. Something was determined that there would be no pictures snapped inside the mansion.

Photographers often shoot instant Polaroids to test the lighting and makeup. "All the Polaroids I shot in the house came out black," Murray said. "I'd shoot with the same camera and the same film outside and the pictures would come out fine. Inside—black. I tried different cameras, different film, everything. It was always the same. Everything I tried to photograph inside that house came out black."

Murray spent most of his time outside setting up shots. The fashion coordinator and the art director spent more time inside ironing, sewing, or experimenting with the clothes and models. From the start, the house exerted a negative force. Then things turned up missing. The coordinator's scissors disappeared. The art director broke out in a cold sweat every time he entered; by the last day, he was literally pouring with perspiration. And, as night began to fall, everyone started to feel more and more uncomfortable.

"Even people who always laughed about ghosts just wanted to get out of there. We all began to feel as though something absolutely terrible would happen to us." Murray described the blanket of dread that covered the small group. "Everyone was so scared. We finished up there ahead of schedule. You never saw a crew pack so fast in your life. Frocks and makeup were flying in every direction. There was something so ominous about the place. We literally fled—ran out of the place. I didn't even wait for the elevator. I ran down seven flights of stairs, hopped in my car and drove away. None of us ever went back." When the fashion coordinator got home, she threw up; and more than a decade later, she still feels so traumatized that she will not talk about her experience in the house.

When pop star Madonna bought Castillo del Lago in 1993, she painted the entire building red with a red-and-white-striped retaining wall—to the great dismay of her neighbors. Other than her refusal to blend in, Madonna ran her "Castle by the Lake" much the way her mobster-forerunner, Bugsy, must have: security guards insured safety and privacy; entrance by invitation only; the finest artwork, furnishings, music and entertainment. Madonna confided to a friend that on occasion, she felt a force throughout the house, a force that was not safe. Some of her guests

Above: Castillo del Lago provided the perfect setting for horror films—too perfect!

had even seen the gray, shadowy figure of a man in a fedora hat—a style popular in Bugsy Siegel's day. If this was the same presence that overpowered Murray and his co-workers, its strength seemed to have diminished a bit, perhaps because of the positive energy Madonna brought with her. In the eighties, when only one person lived in the castle, the spirit had the run of the place. All the energy Madonna and her entourage brought with them forced it to withdraw, no doubt creating resentment. That is why every time Steven, the caretaker Madonna hired, stepped outside, the doors closed and locked behind him, even on the patio. That patio was rimmed with motion-detector lights. More than once, Pete, the feisty, fifty-pound terrier who patrolled the house, barked "for no reason" at the dark end of the patio. Steven checked, said nothing was ever there—but a light always clicked on, sometimes two or three times in an evening. The only reason that could happen was for something to move in proximity to an individual light. And, most unsettling of all, late at night, when he was alone in the cavernous home, Steven could hear a man's voice calling his name.

Carlton Wilborn is an actor and dancer who appeared in Madonna's film *Truth or Dare*. Madonna and Carlton became good friends during the shoot, and Carlton was a frequent visitor to Castillo del Lago. More often than not, he enjoyed the time he spent in the magnificent home. He believed the Bugsy legend after exploring a tunnel that opened into the elevator shaft, a quick escape route for Siegel. He had also heard about the man in the fedora, but never felt fearful in the house…well, *almost* never.

Occasionally, Carlton stayed at the house in Madonna's absence. After one such night in 1994, Carlton headed for the kitchen by way of a long hallway lined with ornate columns. A dark, round table in the center of the hallway held flowers. As Carlton passed this table, he noticed dust. Madonna's staff was thorough, so this was unusual. He stopped to run his finger across it and, to his surprise, found that the dust was *between* the wooden table and its glass top. And in the dust, there was strange writing. Carlton couldn't make it out and none of the staff knew how it got there.

On another occasion, a friend joined Carlton for dinner at the castle. As they walked into the living room, Pete followed. In the center of the living room on a table was an enormous Bible, about a foot high, bound in very ornate metal. Carlton and his friend stood a few feet away, looking at photography books on the bookshelves, when Pete sniffed the air hungrily. He caught a scent that clearly upset him.

Pete walked straight to the Bible, staring at it "super intensely." He tucked his tail between his legs and began whining and crying, all the while his nose touching the Good Book. Unable to turn away, Pete fearfully backed up until he was between Carlton's feet, still staring at the book and crying. Carlton and his friend instinctively focused on the Bible. Just like Tom Murray, they were instantly filled with dread, overwhelmed that something terrible would happen if they stayed in that room. With every fiber of their beings, they believed they should run. "The whole room felt so freaky to us…it felt dark, like an energy I did not want to get close to, ever. We got the hell out of there."

Carlton did not think the evil energy would follow him. Indeed, he and his friend enjoyed a quiet dinner that same evening in another part of the house. Nor did he feel it was attached to Madonna in any way. "I've thought about it many times. I don't know if it was in the house or attached directly to the Bible. It was creepy, without a doubt. I'll never know what was going on there."

The spirit could have emanated from the Bible. Spirits do travel with objects they loved in life. This is the explanation for the "curse" attached to sacred objects removed from burial sites or why Grandma's chair sometimes rocks "by itself." But this presence clearly traveled throughout the house taking objects, locking doors. And it was present before Madonna and her Bible moved in. Was it the spirit of the man in the fedora, a guard to Bugsy Siegel, or even Siegel himself? Firmly rooted in evil, clearly wanting control, it could have been a gangster. Or his deeply vengeful victim. The Material Girl had no desire to find out. She sold the castle in 1997. The spirit now calls a new name in the middle of the night from the castle by the lake.

*

Ciro's and the Comedy Store

mobbed

*T*he ribbon of restaurants and nightclubs that made up the Sunset Strip during its heyday in the 1940s and '50s defined glamour and extravagance. The brightest stars and the biggest movie moguls gathered there to dine, dance and romance. They went to see and be seen, to gossip and be gossiped about. One of the most popular rendezvous was Ciro's. For nearly two decades, the nightclub offered top-flight entertainment to an audience full of celebrities. Today it is The Comedy Store, home to the hottest names in stand-up comedy. But late at night, it's the ghosts of Ciro's who rule the roost.

Facing Page: Mobster Mickey Cohen, 1957, who may have "made" some ghosts at Ciro's.

Ciro's popularity waned in the late '50s, but the building's long tradition of entertainment continued uninterrupted as a rock-and-roll venue in the '60s and, beginning in the mid '70s, as The Comedy Store, now owned and operated by Mitzi Shore, mother of comic Pauly Shore.

I was a cocktail waitress at "the Store" in 1981 and '82. Richard Pryor, in preparation for his film *Live on the Sunset Strip*, performed there every night, drawing celebrities like Bette Midler, Mick Jagger, Peter O'Toole and Sugar Ray Leonard. In the middle of it all, Robin Williams or John Belushi would jump on stage and the place would go wild. The new kids in town—Garry Shandling, Michael Keaton, Arsenio Hall, Richard Belzer, Sam Kinison—stood in the back, awestruck.

When the laughter died out and the last glass was washed, another kind of show began. In the early morning hours, when the club was quiet, the Store was in the hands of comic Blake Clark, who doubled as doorman and security. A charming, funny man from Georgia, once a marine platoon leader in Vietnam, Blake was no shrinking violet. But more than once, he ran for the door without looking back.

Above: Ciro's—the most glamorous nightclub on the Sunset Strip, 1946. **Facing Page:** The Comedy Store today. **Inset:** Interior of the Main Room where Dr. Taff saw three ghosts.

Late one night, Blake checked the large showroom that had been Ciro's main room. He called out to make sure no one was backstage. No answer. He moved to lock up but stopped in his tracks. A chair on one end of the stage was sliding toward the other side. Blake stood frozen as the chair glided effortlessly three feet, ten feet, twenty feet. When he could find his own feet, Blake was gone.

The spirits in that room always gave the late Sam Kinison trouble, constantly messing with the lights and sound equipment while he was on the stage. One night, Sam challenged the spirits to show themselves; all the lights went off. Another time, Blake was closing up the main room and could hear Sam doing his act in the Original Room next door. As Blake waited for another employee, he heard a low buzz of voices: "Bssimm, bssimm, bssimm." Sam got louder, reaching his trademark scream, and the buzzing got louder, too. Blake could now make it out clearly. The voices were chanting angrily, "It's him. It's him. It's him."

Sightings weren't limited to nighttime. One afternoon, as Blake played

a video game in an annex off the kitchen, he felt a man watching from several feet behind him. Out of the corner of his eye, he saw a guy in a brown leather bomber jacket. Finally, Clark turned to acknowledge him. "I could see through him. Then he disappeared," Blake says. "I just ran." Later that afternoon, Debbie Dean, an assistant, walked into her office on the third floor. A man in a brown leather bomber jacket was crouching in terror in a corner near her desk. A moment later, he faded away. When Debbie and Blake compared notes, they were convinced they had seen the same man.

Psychics believe that ghosts often re-create the circumstances of their deaths. If that's true, then it would appear this man met his maker here. The Mob had its fingers in this club back in the '40s and '50s. Gangster Mickey Cohen shook the place down every week. Chances are good someone got bumped off.

That's what Dr. Barry Taff believes. There were so many occurrences at the Store that Debbie called UCLA's parapsychology team in the summer of 1982 and asked them to investigate. Taff and his partners conducted an uneventful exploration of the club until they got to the backstage dressing area of the main room, where Blake had seen the chair move. While the team discussed matters in the back room, two coins materialized from thin air, falling from the ceiling. Taff was excited by that; it was a harbinger.

Later, the group was led to a storage area under the stage. When he entered this basement, Taff fell to the ground, stricken with agonizing

Above Left: Rock Hudson and Phyllis Winger at Ciro's, 1958. **Above Right:** Ciro's patrons included Barbara Stanwyck and Robert Taylor, 1940.

pain in his legs. "If there is something physical to pick up on," he says, "I always feel it." His powerful psychic ability had tapped into the excruciating pain that someone, sometime, had suffered there. He felt strongly that this pain was no accident, that it was purposely inflicted. To Taff, the basement felt like the "heart" of the building, where the Mob carried out evil deeds.

Blake Clark agrees. Around three o'clock one morning, he heard a low, guttural growl emanating from the basement. The metal gate pad-locked across the entrance began to bulge out, as if a tremendous weight was pushing against it. The gate groaned against the weight, then suddenly snapped back to its original position. Standing in front of it was a hulking, amorphous figure, almost seven feet tall, " . . . and so dark it was darker than the blackness behind it. I got this tremendous feeling of malevolence from it." Blake set a new land-speed record leaving the building.

Blake had one last experience in the basement. He went downstairs with another comic, Joey Gaynor. Within seconds, Joey, terrified, held his hands up in front of him, yelling, "Don't come near me! No! Stay away!" Blake looked where Joey was looking but saw nothing. He looked at Joey and could see his breath, as if it were freezing cold; yet, when he touched Joey's hands, they were burning hot. Just then, a piece of black cardboard dropped from the air and hit Blake on the hand. He picked it up and turned it over. His name was written on it. Blake doesn't go to the basement anymore.

In April of 1994, I returned to the Store to film a segment on haunted Hollywood for a local news show. I also invited Taff.

As I went before the camera in the main room, Taff watched the tap-ing, aware of activity and people passing behind him, including three men watching from the back. When we finished, the crew packed up and left. Taff was the last one out. He turned to acknowledge the men. They were all wearing '40s-style suits with wide lapels. And as Taff looked at them, they disappeared.

✳

Beverly Glen

*T*he road that winds through the canyon of Beverly Glen is one of the oldest thoroughfares in the city. A forest of oaks, sycamores and thick greenery, it is still a rustic, scenic route connecting the San Fernando Valley to the west side of Los Angeles. Where cars now hug the curves as they climb toward Mulholland Drive, horses, wagons and coaches once carried passengers on what could be a very long and arduous journey. By the late 1800s, several small inns and way stations had sprung up to accommodate the needs of weary travelers, whether cowboys, farmers . . . or even lovers looking for a remote rendezvous.

Facing Page: Doorway to the haunted 1880s Beverly Glen roadhouse.

Four Oaks Restaurant

a house is not a home

For hundreds of years, a single giant oak tree formed of four separate trunks stood at a spot now about two miles north of Sunset Boulevard. In the 1940s, it was foolishly cut down for parking space before the community could protest. Today, its memory is recalled in the name of a lovely restaurant situated in a century-old house that stood nearby. Once a bordello, Four Oaks remains a favorite haunt for at least one very loyal customer.

Long before gold was discovered in the California hills, local springs fed the flora and carved a winding creek bed that became the Glen's main road. In the 1880s, a small inn and cafe was built in the shade of the big oak. It catered mainly to cowboys and animal herders on their drives to market. By the turn of the century, the little cafe had more business than it could handle.

Facing Page: The upstairs dining area was a brothel at one time. Ghosts were seen both there and downstairs in the original dining area, now the kitchen.

The inn did a thriving business throughout the Prohibition years of the 1920s. Bootleg liquor made on the premises was served to people downstairs at the bar and in the main dining room. It was also served to the men who visited the working women living upstairs, some of whom left behind evidence of their days and nights of pleasure to be discovered decades later.

Current owner and chef Peter Roelant delights in telling of his restaurant's notorious history. He purchased it in 1989 from Jack Allen, an actor who unearthed a treasure trove from the "house" during a renovation in the 1960s. In the walls, he found old lipsticks, small metal boxes with rouge pots, little purses and old wine and whiskey bottles. Downstairs, workers discovered a false shelf hiding a secret compartment; inside was a fully operational still. Behind that was a secret passageway leading to a house up the hill. The remodeling may have yielded an amusing cache, but it also stirred up a former patron of the house.

Sometime after the work was completed, a busboy spent the night at the restaurant. He was awakened by a light in the fireplace behind him. He turned, rubbed his eyes and in an instant was on his feet, screaming. A large glowing figure hovered on the other side of the room. The young man spent the rest of the night outside, refusing to reenter. He quit the next day.

Jack dismissed the occurrence and often stayed in an apartment at the restaurant. The Glen was very "laid-back" in those days, a peaceful place to be. Steve McQueen and his motorcycle pals loved to ride up the winding road and hang out at Four Oaks with other celebrity locals like Vincent Price, Elke Sommer and her husband, writer Joe Hyams. Late one evening, Jack was startled awake by a noise. He got out of bed to investigate, but no sooner had his feet hit the floor than his bedroom door flew open. A form radiating light entered the room. Terrified, Jack jumped up on his bed and screamed, "You don't belong here. Go away! Go away! Go away!" The glowing form stood still for a time, as if confused about what to do. After a while, it disappeared, and Jack never saw it again. He considered the building's colorful past and decided it must have been someone who died of pleasure—or was returning for it.

Today, people return to Four Oaks for the good food, and the only spirits have corks in them. And though the tree is gone, its memory still blankets the house in the shade of the past.

✳

The Headless Ghost of Beverly Glen

the lover and the landowner

*N*ow boarded up, a three-story structure on North Beverly Glen, reputed to be one of the oldest buildings in the Glen was a roadhouse more than a century ago. Many past tenants also believe it to be the site of one of the most gruesome crimes in history.

In the mid '60s, long after the roadhouse had been converted into apartments, UCLA students Mel Sherer and Nancy Macjeski shared the top floor. Two other tenants lived on the ground floor. The middle apartment was empty.

Mel and Nancy were awakened several times by the sound of footsteps running up the stairs, accompanied by heavy breathing. The footsteps would stop at the door of their apartment, and suddenly the air around them would turn cold and clammy. A dark, ominous feeling would pervade the room; the frightened couple would huddle together until it dissipated. They told their neighbors, but no one downstairs had heard

Facing Page: Two ghosts linger in this 1880s roadhouse. One is the husband, the other the lover...one is the killer, the other the victim.

or felt anything unusual; and there were no inside stairs linking
the apartments.

One night, Mel was upstairs with one of his neighbors when Nancy
came home on her motor scooter. She scrambled up the outside stairs
and burst into the apartment. "I saw a terrible thing!" she shrieked.
"It was horrible!" Gasping for breath, she told them that as she parked
her scooter, she had caught sight of something in her rear view mirror.
Nancy turned around but saw nothing. Yet when she looked again in
the mirror, the image was still there. She bolted upstairs.

Mel was standing by the window. "Did it look like a man dressed completely in yellow, with no head?"

"How did you know?" Nancy asked, incredulous.

Mel motioned her and the neighbor to the window. Three stories below
was a terrible sight indeed. The glowing form of a man dressed in an
opera cape, all in yellow except for a black tie, stood by the side of the
road. His head was gone. "Our hearts started to beat fast, and we really had to work to calm ourselves down," Mel says. "We stared at it for
about fifteen minutes. Then it disappeared."

When the landlord came by the next day, he asked in an off-handed
way, "By the way, has the ghost shown up yet?" From their expres-
sions, he could tell that it had. He went on to recount the story of the
headless man in yellow.

Like the apartment house, the original inn had also been divided into
three floors. On the ground floor, beyond the porch where riders took
off their gear, was the kitchen and dining room. The second floor was
the main room or lobby. The top floor was made up of small bed-
rooms. Stairs connected all three floors, but they were walled in when
the building was converted to apartments.

Around the turn of the century, a wealthy landowner occasionally
brought his attractive wife into the city for an evening at the theater.

Afterward, they would sleep at the inn.

Sometimes the wife would make the journey alone. On one such trip, she was smitten by a young dandy, a man known for his outlandish style of dress and his favorite color—yellow. They began to meet regularly, and always stayed at the inn.

Eventually, a friend told the cuckolded husband where he could find the lovers together. Grabbing a scythe, the irate man mounted his horse and rode like Death across the Valley to the inn. The frightened innkeeper could only point toward the third floor. Charging past him up the steps, the husband burst into the room—the same room Mel and Nancy slept in. As his wife screamed, he raised the blade and cut off the head of her lover. He was later executed for this murder, and the widow inherited his vast estate. Since then, the lover has been seen waiting on the road for the woman he loved.

Mel and Nancy were astonished . . . and still frightened. They felt such anger in those footsteps—the husband's presence—and wanted to make them go away. They decided to conduct an exorcism and invited several friends experienced in the occult to join them. Protected by cloves of garlic, the group shouted the key phrase, "What in God's name do you want?" Miraculously, Mel and Nancy never heard the footsteps again.

In 1972, a young actress named Corinne Broskette moved into the ground-floor apartment. New tenants were on the third floor, and a photographer who worked for David Bowie lived in the middle. Gradually, Corinne became aware of a ghostly presence living with her that had a way of comforting her when she was sad—someone who stroked her hair when a love affair was on the rocks. After learning the story of the inn, she came to believe that this presence was the spirit of the lover.

"It was always a warm feeling—I was never afraid," Corinne stresses. She's sure it was the lover, because he acted like a lover in every way. Sometimes, when she was preparing to go out, he would hide her keys

so she couldn't leave. And once, he followed her into her car. As she
drove down the canyon road toward Sunset Boulevard, Corinne
advised the spirit to return to the inn. "The city has changed. Once I
leave the canyon, it will be very confusing. You might get lost and not
be able to find your way back," she warned him. Instantly, he left the
car and went home.

Everyone in the building knew the story of the murder and had
encountered the lover at one time or another. What's more, after the
photographer uncovered the steps in his section of the building, everyone could hear the footsteps of the husband again.

"We all felt his rage," says Corinne. She also believes she him heard
sobbing outside her window one night—deep, deep sobs coming from
the front porch area. "I think when he first got to the inn and discovered that his wife was cheating on him, he broke down." The spirit of
the wife has never been felt.

In 1974, Jill Place shared Corinne's apartment for several months.
Like Corinne, Jill felt quite welcomed by the spirit. Not only did he
stroke her hair, but he sometimes climbed right into her bed, curling
up next to her and cuddling close. She was never afraid of him. No one
was.

Today, the property is in great decline. No one has lived there for
years, and weeds and vines grow wild on the grounds. No one can tell
us if the husband still makes his nightly charge up the stairs. And no
one comes for the tender lover to comfort and hold. Forgotten and
alone, the headless man may be there still, waiting by the roadside for
his lady to return.

※

hollywood
haunts

Hollywood Haunts includes three different places where film folk congregated, and so do their ghosts—studios, theaters and the city's grand old hotels.

Every good theater has a resident ghost. Whether on stage or behind it, in the audience or in the projection booth, lovers of entertainment bring an intensity of emotion to their favorite theater night after night. Some return to the place itself to recapture the thrill of emotion they once felt there.

Courageous adventurers built the first movie studios in the first decade of the century. Shunned by conservative locals, the "movies"—as the people who worked in them came to be called—looked to one another for friendship and recreation. To be an employee of a studio was to be part of a family. It is their voices still heard in offices, their shadows cast upon stages, their footsteps pacing the dressing rooms.

Hollywood hotels hold great romance—so many rooms with so many secrets—four walls that have seen and heard so much. As you walk through the corridors of an old hotel, you can almost feel the past walking alongside. In Hollywood's haunted hotels, there's no "almost" about it.

The Studios

*M*ore than twenty years ago, co-author Marc Wanamaker interviewed security guards and employees at nearly a dozen studios—mostly old-timers who had been on their respective lots for decades. Almost all of them are dead now, but their stories—plus a few of our own—live on in Hollywood Haunts.

Facing Page: Paramount Studios, 5555 Melrose Avenue. Spirits from the neighboring Hollywood Memorial Cemetery have been seen coming through the walls into Paramount Studios. **Above:** Pioneering comedy producer Al Christy was ranked with comedy giants Mack Sennett and Hal Roach. Christie, in white, breaks ground in 1928 at the Metropolitan Studios. Also pictured, comedian Harold Lloyd (fourth from right) and Howard Hughes (far right).

Culver Studios

*P*ioneer filmmaker Thomas Ince's impact on Hollywood history was so enormous that the French called him film's first prophet. He set production ideals to which the industry aspired for years to come. Sadly, though, he is remembered more for his death than for his tremendous contribution to the art and craft of movie-making.

Ince died in November 1924, while celebrating his forty-third birthday aboard William Randolph Hearst's yacht. The abruptness of his death and his stature in the industry generated a series of sensational rumors. The most enduring is that Hearst caught his mistress, Marion Davies, kissing Charlie Chaplin and shot at him, accidentally hitting and killing Ince. The small party on board—including Louella

Facing Page: Pioneer producer Thomas Ince wearing the "funny bowler hat" workers saw on his ghost. **Above:** Ince at his desk in 1920.

Parsons, who later made a deal with Hearst for a syndicated gossip column—was sworn to secrecy.

The visionary producer-director-writer built what is now Culver Studios in 1918. The lot changed hands several times after his death, with each owner bringing a new and distinct era. Cecil B. De Mille, Howard Hughes, David O. Selznick, Desi Arnaz and Lucille Ball all made significant contributions to film and television history on this lot. *Gone With the Wind, King Kong, Citizen Kane, E.T.* and television's *The Untouchables, Lassie, Hogan's Heroes* and *Batman* are just a few of the classics that were shot here.

Rumors about hauntings have persisted for years. Employees report ghostly security guards patrolling the lot at night. Others recount seeing the ghost of a man climb the stairs in the main administration building to the executive screening room, originally Ince's private projection room, on the second floor. And guards on the third floor have

been frightened by the apparition of a woman from time to time. She disappears quickly, leaving a cold spot or chilling wind in her wake.

Remodeling can be extremely irritating or upsetting to a spirit. Just prior to some major reconstruction in 1988, Ince's ghost began to reveal his displeasure. The first to encounter him were two workers who reported seeing a man in an odd, bowler-type hat watching them from the catwalks above Stage 1-2-3. When they spoke to him, he turned and walked through the second-floor wall.

Later that summer, special-effects man Eugene Hilchey was swapping stories with a worker who had seen a man wearing an odd hat, this time on Stage 2-3-4. Hilchey thought the ghost might fit the description of Ince. What the worker said next convinced him that it was indeed him. The spirit had turned to the worker and, in no uncertain terms told him, "I don't like what you're doing to my studio." Then he disappeared through a wall.

Much of Ince's original lot was saved, and the sense of history is very strong. Today, Culver Studios is one of the busiest lots in town. Let's hope the indomitable spirit of Mr. Ince finds some peace in that.

※

Facing Page: Ince in his Galleon Room, which was hidden behind secret panels near his office. His ghost has been seen here too. **Above:** Interior of Stage One just before it was demolished in 1988. Ince was heard in the catwalks moments before the wrecking ball hit. (photo: Eugene Hilchey)

Universal Studios

Universal Studios was home to the masters of horror and suspense. **Dracula, Frankenstein, The Invisible Man, The Wolf Man, The Mummy** *all were immortalized here with the help of stars like Bela Lugosi, Boris Karloff, Claude Rains, Lon Chaney and his son, Lon Chaney Jr.*

One of Chaney Sr.'s greatest triumphs was 1925's *The Phantom of the Opera*. Universal built Stage 28 for the spectacular production, which became an immediate classic.

Facing Page: Lon Chaney as Death at the masked ball in *The Phantom of the Opera*.
Above: The front gates of Universal, 1936

Studio folklore tells of a ghostly man in a dark cape sighted on Stage 28. Over the years, electricians, carpenters, designers, art directors and guards have all reported strange goings-on there. Even people who didn't know the history of the stage reported seeing a man in a cape running on the catwalks. And guards admitted being "spooked" by doors opening and closing and lights going on and off on that empty stage in the middle of the night.

Could it be Lon Chaney running on the catwalks overhead? Fact or fable, it's all part of the legend of Universal's most talked-about sound stage.

✳

Facing Page, Top: The sets for the opera house were so huge, a special stage was built for them in 1923. Stage 28 still houses the sets and, some say, the Phantom. **Bottom Right:** Bela Lugosi and Boris Karloff vied for the crown of King of Terror, which they inherited from the all-time master, Lon Chaney. **Middle Left:** Patrons of the Paris opera house gasp in terror at the Phantom. The magnificent set is a permanent fixture on the lot. **Bottom Left:** Lon Chaney as the Phantom. **Above:** Lon Chaney's success spanned fifteen years, until 1930, at forty-seven, when he lost his life to cancer.

Raleigh Studios

*R*aleigh Studios, built in 1914, has a rich history that includes names like Dolores Del Rio, Hopalong Cassidy, Charlie Chaplin, Frank Sinatra and Kevin Costner.

In 1932, an electrician fell to his death from the catwalk on Stage 5. For more than sixty years, stagehands have felt his presence, and there are continuous reports of power failures, movement of heavy equipment and drastic drops in temperature. Two security guards have even heard music coming mysteriously from the walls.

Studio employee Don Kane remembers a specific incident in 1972, as he locked Stage 5 on a Sunday night about ten. "I called out, 'Is there anybody in here?' and it was quiet." Kane was almost out the door when he heard a voice shout back from the catwalk. He looked up toward the rafters. The work light, mounted five feet from the catwalk and weighing close to three hundred pounds, began to swing in an arc of six to eight feet. Kane again called out, but no one answered. He turned to his assistant. "You did hear a voice, right?" The assistant nodded. Kane, nervous, backed up, closed the door and walked away.

In 1994, we took three parapsychologists there. Dr. Barry Taff, Barry Conrad and Jeanette Batton knew no details, only that Stage 5 was purported to be haunted. The second they stepped onto the stage, all three felt an intense sensation of falling over backward. Taff even grabbed my arm to catch himself. They were convinced something was wrong with the floor ... until we told them of the spirit who haunts Stage 5.

✳

Facing Page: Notorious Stage 5, haunted for over sixty years. **Inset:** As Tec Art Studio, 1928.

Theaters

*D*ecades ago, going to the movies was a special event, and Hollywood's theaters reflected that in their distinctive architecture. Our first haunted theater, designed as a Moorish palace, houses the ghost of a movie pioneer cheated of his greatest success. The ghost of Howard Hughes has been spotted in a magnificent Art Deco theater he once owned. And one of Hollywood's oldest legitimate theaters has so many ghosts that customers complain about all the noise in the balcony.

Facing Page: The spectacular main auditorium of Grauman's Chinese Theater. **Above:** The Warner Pacific theater on opening night.

The Pacific Theater

you can't cheat an honest man

*I*n the lobby of this grand theater is a plaque dedicated to the
memory of Sam Warner, one of the four Warner Brothers, who

died suddenly on the very eve of the success of which they all dreamed.

Death cheated Sam Warner of the fruits of his labors. But Sam would

not be cheated.

Facing Page: The Warner Brothers Theater. **Above:** The tribute to Sam Warner on the theater's opening night program read: *1887-1927 To our beloved brother, Samuel L. Warner, who conceived and planned it, but who was summoned before completion of his work, this Warner Brothers Theater is dedicated...a memorial of the beauty and pleasure he sought always to hold out to humanity which he so greatly loved...he was there in spirit.*

In the late '20s, after several successes and nearly as many failures, the four Warner brothers–Harry, Albert, Sam and Jack–risked everything they had on the production of a new movie, a talkie–a musical called *The Jazz Singer*. As chief executive of Warner Brothers Studios, Sam was instrumental in the development of sound. He also insisted on Al Jolson over George Raft and George Jessel for the lead.

While *The Jazz Singer* was being filmed, Warner Brothers raced to complete its new flagship theater—the largest movie house ever built in Hollywood—with Sam personally supervising installation of the sound system for the risky film's West Coast premiere. The brothers sweated out the buzz around town that talking pictures were nothing more than a passing fad. Between production of the movie and construction delays on the theater, Sam barely slept. When it was obvious his new theater would not be ready in time to debut the film, Sam stood in the lobby and cursed it.

The Jazz Singer opened in New York on October 6, 1927, to ecstatic crowds and rave reviews. But none of the brothers were there. Twenty-four hours before the premiere, forty-year-old Sam suffered a cerebral hemorrhage and died in Los Angeles. His brothers left New York before the premiere.

Hollywood history was made that October night, and the course of movie-making changed forever. Sam Warner's theater opened six months later, on April 29, 1928, with an inconsequential film starring Conrad Nagel called *The Glorious Betsy*. Al Jolson emceed. The brothers placed a plaque honoring Sam's memory in the lobby. That night, with their hearts and minds focused on Sam, the brothers no doubt felt he was there with them in spirit—and he probably was. A man as driven as Sam Warner could not leave this earth with his work still unfinished.

Since that night, there have been random sightings of Sam at the theater and in the administration offices above. Area residents have reported seeing him pace the lobby over the spot where he once stood and cursed. And late one night a quarter century ago, two men on the cleaning crew saw Sam walk right across the lobby to the elevator. When it arrived, Sam got on and pushed the button. The door closed and the elevator went up. When a security guard made his rounds through the lobby, the terrified men told him what they'd seen, then quit on the spot. The guard was not bothered by the story. He only wondered why Sam bothered with an elevator. Why didn't he just "float" to the upstairs offices?

Current employees of the security company protecting the building are quite familiar with Sam. When things are quiet, they can hear him in the offices above the theater, moving chairs or scratching at the door. And for as long as they have been there, the elevator has gone up and down "by itself."

The theater is slated to be restored to its original glory as the Hollywood Entertainment Museum, dedicated to the arts of motion pictures, radio, television and recording. What a glorious fate for this landmark theater! Sam Warner must be very proud.

✳

Facing Page: The Warner Brothers—Sam, Harry, Jack and Al, 1921. **Above:** The Warner Brothers Theater. **Inset:** The theater's lush interior.

The Pantages Theater

howard's end

*H*oward Hughes was an enigma—aviator, movie-maker, inventor, playboy and, in the end, sad recluse. But in Hollywood, he was happy for a time. Perhaps that's why he's back . . .

Hollywood's last glorious movie palace was also the last to bear the name of the great theater-circuit mogul Alexander Pantages. The Pantages is an Art Deco masterpiece, still considered one of the most beautiful theaters in the world.

In 1949, Howard Hughes acquired the Pantages as part of his national theater chain when he bought RKO Pictures. He set up plush offices on the second floor, where Pantages and his two sons had their offices.

Facing Page: The lavish lobby where every detail is a work of art. **Above:** Is it Alexander Pantages or Howard Hughes whose footsteps are heard in the auditorium?

The mysterious—and by this time tyrannical—millionaire sold his stock in RKO in the mid '50s and withdrew from public life completely a decade later.

In 1967, Pacific Theaters bought the Pantages and later joined forces with the Nederlander Corporation, working to restore the place to its original splendor and turn it into a legitimate house for Broadway

touring companies. Since 1992, Karla Rubin has been executive assistant to the president of Nederlander, with offices on the second floor. From the beginning, she has felt a presence, primarily in the conference room, which had been Hughes' office. "There's something about the temperature of the room—a coldness," she says. "I always feel a wind go past me when there's no air-conditioning on." Rubin has also heard a lot of bumping and banging and the clicking of the brass handles on the desk drawers. And every once in a while, a cold wind blows through the executive suite, accompanied by the faint smell of cig-

arettes. Twice she has caught sight of an apparition—a very tall man she believes to be Hughes. Dressed inconspicuously, he is always rounding a corner in the remodeled suite where his original office door used to be.

In 1990, vandals broke into the theater and damaged the upper balcony area. "After that happened," says Tiffany Peterson, the Pantages' house manager for the past seven years, "there was a lot of activity on the second floor. It seemed like someone was really mad or upset. Things were really banging around."

Then there's the legend of the singing woman that Peterson believes dates from 1932, when a female patron died in the mezzanine during a

show. Some time after her death, when the auditorium was dark and quiet, the voice of a woman could be heard singing . . . sometimes during the day, other times late at night after everyone had gone home. Employees have developed a theory about the voice. The unfortunate woman may have been an aspiring singer who'd come to see one of the musicals so popular in the early '30s. Though she'd died in the theater as a spectator, perhaps she continues to live out her dream of performing at the Pantages. Over the years, she seems to have lost some of her stage fright. Recently, her voice was picked up on a microphone and carried over the monitor during a live performance.

Earlier this year, a wardrobe lady was the last to leave the darkened theater. As she walked toward a side exit in the auditorium, the emergency lights along the aisles went out. Thrust into complete darkness, she stumbled and bumped into something. She became disoriented and couldn't find her way out. In the darkness, someone took her elbow, helped her up and guided her with a firm hand toward the door. She opened it, letting in some light. The grateful woman then turned to thank her rescuer, but no one was there.

✳

Facing Page: Alexander Pantages. **Above:** The RKO Pantages, 1953.

The Palace

let the good times roll

id you ever have such a wonderful night that you wished it would never end? Or maybe there's one you'd like to relive just one more time . . . or ten more times . . . or twenty? The Palace has provided many such nights for the young and old alike. Folks have been flocking here for almost seventy years. And a few don't want to go home.

It opened in 1927 as the Hollywood Playhouse, one of four legitimate theaters in Hollywood. Over the years, it has been home to Fanny Brice's Baby Snooks radio show, Ken Murray's famed Blackouts theater revue and such television shows as *This Is Your Life*, *The Hollywood Palace*, *The Lawrence Welk Show*, *The Merv Griffin Show* and many Bob Hope specials.

Since then, the Palace has been remodeled as an ornate nightclub, the site of television specials, premiere parties and film locations and a showcase for top music artists. With such a list of credits past and present, there's no question that the Palace has played host to more stars than any other theater in Hollywood, while at the same time providing thousands of people with some very special memories. Some of them, it seems, have come back for more.

Facing Page: Ken Murray between two Old Gold Girls (photo: Gene Lester).

Before the Palace installed a sophisticated alarm system, Dwayne Soto, a rather large and imposing fellow, used to patrol the premises at night—and any one of his experiences would be enough for most people.

The first occurred about 2:30 one spring morning in 1992. Dwayne was making his rounds through the club's three stories when he heard some jazzy piano music. He checked downstairs for a radio but found none. He climbed the stairs to the first landing and listened. Someone was definitely playing the piano upstairs, "beautiful music," Dwayne says, "like I never heard before." He followed it to the third floor and the smaller Comedy Room.

Some kind of light was emanating from the room, but he couldn't tell what it was. He tried the door. It was locked, and there was no other entrance to the room. He paused, listening to the music. Silently, he slipped the key in the door. When he opened it, the music stopped instantly. Dwayne saw no one. He looked at the piano. Normally, it was closed and covered, the bench tucked away. But now, the cover was off, the keyboard was open and the bench was pulled out. Dwayne ran downstairs, let himself out and stayed there for the remainder of his shift. Now he remembers the experience with longing. "It was so beautiful. I wish I could hear it again, but I never have."

Weeks later, Dwayne was locking up the second-floor lobby when he got a strange feeling. Suddenly, a cold wind blew, and a beautiful perfume filled the air. He moved toward the stairs. That's when he distinctly felt someone tap him on the shoulder. He turned, but no one was there—just the cold wind and the fragrance. "It was really neat," Dwayne says with a smile.

Above: The El Capitan, featuring Ken Murray's Blackouts, the longest-running revue in the history of L.A.'s legitimate theater, 1942-1949. **Facing Page:** The Hollywood Playhouse, 1928.

On another evening, Dwayne brought Sarge, his cousin's German shepherd, with him. Again, it was about 2:30 and all was quiet. Dwayne was reading the paper at one of the tables; Sarge lay quietly at his feet. Suddenly, the dog picked up its head and stared at the left end of the stage. Dwayne looked where the dog looked. Sarge barked once, and Dwayne released him from his leash. Then he picked up a shotgun, cocked it and followed Sarge toward the stage-left curtain. It moved slightly, and Dwayne saw a figure. A man in a tuxedo was watching him. Dwayne noticed two things about the man right away: He had no feet, and his face was transparent.

"Get him, Sarge!" he commanded, and Sarge took off, but just as he arrived at his destination, the man disappeared. Sarge sniffed the ground. Dwayne looked, but the man was gone.

Shaken, Dwayne set a booby trap in the kitchen. He put a plate on the floor and placed a wine glass on top of it. If someone ran through the room, chances were good he'd kick it over. Then he and Sarge went back to the main room.

At 5:35 a.m., Dwayne and Sarge heard a noise, and both took off for the kitchen. Sarge quickly disappeared behind the door, but a few moments later he reappeared, whining like a puppy. The dog stuck close to Dwayne's leg as he cautiously approached the kitchen and slowly opened the door. The room was  empty. Dwayne looked at his trap. The plate was now resting on top of the wine glass. Dwayne again spent the rest of the night outside . . . this time with Sarge.

There's a reason Dwayne didn't see the apparition's feet. Ghosts often don't recognize remodeling; they see rooms as they were when they lived in them. The man in the tux may have been standing on the original theater floor, beneath the nightclub's dance floor.

Early in 1994, Dwayne was walking on the main dance floor. He was alone in the club, and it was absolutely still. He looked up to the balcony and was surprised to see two older people deep in conversation. "Excuse me," he called out. "You can't be up there." The couple ignored him. Dwayne hurried upstairs and out onto the balcony. The couple was still there. He walked toward them, continuing to call out, but they paid him no attention. Dwayne noticed their old-fashioned, 1930's style clothing. When he got within fifty feet of them, they disappeared. Perhaps the couple was reliving a special anniversary they celebrated there. Whatever the occasion, these lovebirds never seem to run out of things to say. Palace patrons complain regularly of people in the balcony talking and laughing during the show.

Sean Dobbs, operations manager at the Palace, is hard-pressed to believe in ghosts, yet he can't deny what he saw around four o'clock one morning in November of 1993. The band Belly had played to a packed house earlier, but the club was empty and completely dark as Sean and the security chief walked through the main room to secure the building. Afterward, the security chief went home, leaving Sean alone.

When Sean came back out to the nightclub, all the white stage lights were on. A sheer white curtain hung across the stage between him and the lights. He trotted down and looked behind it, wondering who had turned on the lights. Worse, how was he going to turn them off?

Inset: The Palace, July 1952.

The second he had the thought, however, the lights went out. He froze. A few blue lights shone eerily from a catwalk above. Instinctively, Sean started backing away across the dance floor, convinced that someone was playing a trick on him. But he was completely alone.

As he continued watching the stage, he saw something floating in the upper right corner. The blue lights backlit the stage just enough for him to see its shadow on the curtain. It appeared to be a shimmering, wavy mass about five feet square—like a jellyfish, changing all the time. A shiver went up his spine. The mass moved off to the side and disappeared. Sean held his breath; everything was dead still. And then it came back, traveling slowly across the stage. He could see the lights through it. It floated back to where he first saw it and disappeared.

"It was like watching something through water," Sean explains. "It was fluctuating. It was like something on *Star Trek*. I've never seen anything like it."

Maybe the being Sean saw on the stage was trying to send a message. The Palace has had trouble with virtually every piece of electronic equipment at some point in time. And on a fairly regular basis, the adding machines and cash registers print out weird, indecipherable messages during the night, composed of numbers grouped to look like words and sentences. Sean doesn't have any idea what they mean, but he saves all of them.

Who knows? Perhaps they are messages from beyond—from the piano player, the man in the tux, the elderly couple or any number of spirits as yet unseen. The Palace is a place where memories were made. You can't blame people for wanting the good times back. If Sean decodes those messages, he might discover it's a call for another round of drinks in the balcony.

✳

Hotels

*E*ach of our haunted hostelries is distinctly different, and each represents a special chapter of Hollywood history. One, built near the turn of the century, goes back to the earliest days of the movie industry in Los Angeles. Another, Hollywood's first grand hotel, will bring you face to face with Montgomery Clift, Marilyn Monroe and an array of former celebrity guests. And in the epilogue, the Oban Hotel, home to many a struggling actor on the way up—and the way down—provided dramatic proof of the paranormal.

Facing Page: Chateau Marmont, the Castle on the Hill. Its loving, protective spirits either accept you or reject you.

The Alexandria Hotel
the lady in black

*T*oday, at the corner of Fifth and Spring streets in the center of downtown Los Angeles, stands a faded remnant of Hollywood's rich past. Hundreds of people pass it daily, unaware that Churchill, Bernhardt, Caruso, Chaplin, Paderewski, King Edward VIII, Presidents Taft, Wilson and Theodore Roosevelt and dozens more of the world's most powerful and talented personalities were once familiar names on the guest register. And at least one early guest may still wander the halls.

Facing Page: The Alex, circa 1945. The $2 million hotel was so popular that an eleven-story annex was added to the original seven stories just three years after it opened in 1906.

The once-majestic Alexandria Hotel catered to the professional and social needs of the business community of 1906 Los Angeles. With several theaters and restaurants in the area, the Alexandria became a natural meeting place for the newly arriving movie crowd. By 1910, one needed go no further than the lobby to find virtually everyone of importance in the business. This is where the power lunch and networking were born.

As Los Angeles developed in a westerly direction, the movie colony abandoned the Alex for the newer, more modern Biltmore and Ambassador hotels. The once-grand hotel became a ghost of its former self. And so it remained for nearly half a century.

In the early '70s, the hotel received a two-million-dollar facelift. Two actresses strolling downtown on a summer afternoon ventured inside to see where so much history had preceded them. But Nancy Malone and Lisa Mitchell were disappointed to find not a single reference to the history of Hollywood there. They lamented the omission to the owner, who was so impressed by the women's breadth of knowledge that he hired them to help bring that flavor back.

Above: In the Alex's main dining room in 1919, D.W. Griffith, Mary Pickford, Charlie Chaplin and Douglas Fairbanks changed the direction of the movie industry by announcing the formation of their own independent company, United Artists, giving them creative and financial control over their films.

Nancy and Lisa named rooms for the hotel's famous residents and decorated them with portraits of the stars. In the hallways, they hung photographs of Hollywood during the hotel's heyday.

"I believe the past leaves its energy in places, and I'm very respectful of that," says Nancy, a director and Emmy-winning actress. "We were thrilled to be dealing with all that treasure."

After weeks of work, Nancy felt comfortable and safe in the hotel. She had heard stories about a ghost haunting the halls, but as she worked alone at 2 a.m. one September morning, a ghost was the last thing she expected to see. While hanging pictures at the end of a long hallway, she paused and glanced up. There at the end of the hall was a woman dressed in black from head to foot, wearing a large "cartwheel" hat.

"Her dress was beautiful," Nancy recalls, "with an almost bustle back, and the hat had a veil. She seemed to be a woman in her thirties or forties. In that fleeting moment, I saw her walk about eight feet. Her walk and her carriage were beautiful, more like a glide. I didn't see through her, but she wasn't a solid, either. It wasn't like things you see

Above: In his autobiography, Chaplin called it "the swankiest hotel in town...marble columns and crystal chandeliers adorned the lobby, in the center of which was the fabulous 'million dollar carpet'–the mecca of big movie deals."

in the movies—you know, ecto-plasm floating in the air—nor was it a human being. It was something in between."

Nancy remembers a feeling of sadness, a sense that this woman was looking for something. Though she never felt threatened, the experience did shake her up a bit.

"I'm not a ghostbuster," Nancy tells me. "I'm very rooted in reality, but I'm also accepting of mystical events in the world that seem to have no apparent explanation. I believe in a lot of what we don't know about officially. I never got over seeing the ghost. Nearly twenty-five years later, I still remember every detail."

This particular spirit sounds as if she might have been a resident of the hotel in its earliest years. Dressed in black, she could be in mourning. Grief is a powerful emotion; some people have died of it. Maybe that's the story of this poor spirit: stricken with grief, she barely noticed her own passing and continued to grieve, uninterrupted, for more than seventy years. Lost in her emotion, the woman wanders the halls of the Alexandria in search of her lost loved one. Perhaps . . . perhaps not.

✳

Facing Page Above: A 1939 brochure. **Inset:** A postcard advertising the Peacock Room. **Above:** The Gentlemen's Grill was for men only (note spitoon). Bandleader Paul Whiteman got his start playing the piano here.

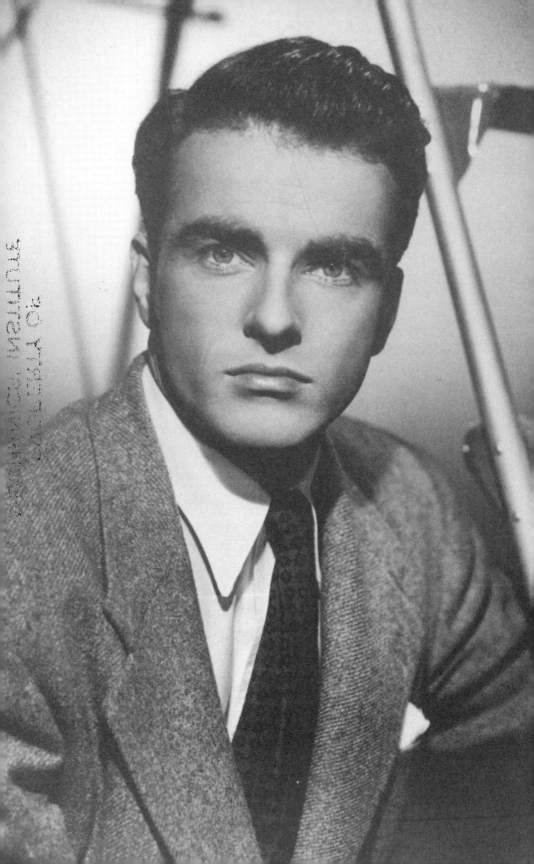

The Hollywood Roosevelt Hotel

marilyn, monty and more…

*W*hen you ask the staff at the Hollywood Roosevelt if it's haunted, the answer is an emphatic yes. In fact, they're quite proud of their ghosts, which is fortunate, because in this celebrated hotel there's an abundance of apparitions to be found, from the boiler room to the roof.

Facing Page: Montgomery Clift seems to be a permanent guest at the hotel. **Above**: The Blossom Room party for *Murder at the Vanities* with Toby Wing on the left and Katherine DeMille on the right, 1934.

As the film business grew and people flocked to Hollywood, local residents saw the need for a prestigious hotel. The city's reigning king and queen, Douglas Fairbanks and Mary Pickford, helped make the Hollywood Roosevelt a reality, and the grand opening of the luxury hotel in 1927 hosted the biggest stars of the day, among them John Gilbert, Gloria Swanson, Greta Garbo, Will Rogers and Clara Bow.

In 1984, the historic hotel underwent a twelve-million-dollar restoration, bringing back its original glory, and with it some old friends. Since the renovations, ghosts have been coming out of the woodwork.

Two weeks prior to the 1985 grand reopening, a spirit was discovered in the Blossom Room, a ballroom that hosted the first Academy Awards banquet in 1929. The spirit took the form of a cold spot—a circle about thirty inches in diameter and more than ten degrees cooler than the rest of the room. Psychics have felt the presence of a man in black who is suffering great anxiety. Perhaps a tuxedoed Academy Award nominee waiting for the envelope?

On that same day, an employee dusting a mirror in the manager's office saw the reflection of a blonde. She turned to speak to the woman, but there was no one standing behind her. Yet when she turned back to the mirror, the reflection was still there. This mirror hung in Suite 1200 often used by Marilyn Monroe. Two psychics have "read" the mirror and felt great sadness. Parapsychologists believe that long after a spirit departs, intense emotion and energy can remain. It's possible that some of Marilyn's sadness is reflected— indeed, trapped—in her mirror.

As guests arrived at the newly refurbished hotel, the staff was alerted to more inexplicable activity. They frequently heard complaints about loud talking in a room next door or children playing in the hallway. When security personnel checked, though, they found the hallways clear and the rooms unoccupied. Phones were lifted from receivers in empty suites two or three times in an evening. A lobby maid was pushed into a supply closet by unseen hands. Other employees reported strange shadows; many refused to work on the ninth floor at all, saying there was "something strange," particularly in and around Room 928 at the end of the hall.

Actor Montgomery Clift lived in Room 928 for three months in 1952, while filming *From Here to Eternity*. He often paced the hallway, rehearsing his lines and practicing the bugle. Maids have felt something cold brush by them in that section, while others have felt a strong presence watching them or walking at their side. On a November night in 1992, an overnight guest in Room 928 felt a hand patting her shoulder while she lay in bed reading. She turned to say goodnight to her husband, but he was sound asleep.

In 1989, a television film crew planned a shoot at the hotel, but the ghosts wreaked havoc with their equipment. As the crew set up cameras outside Clift's room, the house lights went out. When they finally came back on, the sound equipment broke down. Then the lights went out again ... and the film jammed inside the camera. When the crew tried to shoot the Monroe mirror, the smoke alarm went off. And in the

Facing Page: Inset: Roosevelt Hotel, 1942. **Above:** Marilyn Monroe's image has been seen in a mirror in the lobby.

Blossom Room, the cold spot caused the audio equipment to malfunction.

In 1990, a couple strolling on the mezzanine followed piano music out onto a balcony overlooking the deserted Blossom Room. They saw a man in a white suit standing next to a piano. He did not respond to their greeting, and when the couple walked closer, he disappeared. A thorough search was done, but no man in a white suit was found.

Two days later, a hotel engineer, working on the third floor directly above the mezzanine, glanced down the hall and saw a man wearing a white suit and "old shoes." The engineer called out to him but got no answer. The engineer walked closer, to within three feet, and asked the man if he needed help. As he watched, astounded, the man in white walked right through the fire door.

In the spring of 1992, psychic Peter James conducted a series of midnight investigations. In the Academy Room—originally the hotel library and the room used for meetings of civic or social groups—James found a very cold spot, which he described as a tubular shaft that spirits used as an opening to enter this plane. Apparently, this

Above: The Blossom Room and the second Academy Awards banquet, 1930. **Facing Page:** The two-story lobby with a lush Spanish interior and hand-painted wood beams where the ghost of a child was seen playing at the fountain.

room was their gathering place, too. James also encountered the ghost of a little girl who said her name was Carol or Caroline and that she was looking for her mother.

In the penthouse library, James encountered Caroline again. She was crying, so he tried to comfort the child. She was afraid her mother had been hurt. As James tried to learn more, Caroline said she had to find her mommy and vanished.

Several months later, the PBX operator found a delightful little girl playing in the lobby in the early morning. She was about five years old, dressed in a pink jacket and blue jeans. Her light brown hair was pulled back in a ponytail that bounced as she sang and skipped around the fountain. As a man crossed to the front desk, she followed. "Is that your little girl?" the operator asked. The man looked perplexed. When the operator looked back at the child, she had evaporated. Another Caroline sighting?

James felt the "impressions" of many celebrities throughout the hotel grounds: Monroe near her favorite suite by the pool; Errol Flynn, Betty Grable and Edward Arnold in the Blossom Room; Gypsy Rose Lee and Ethel Merman in the poolside Tropicana Bar. Humphrey Bogart, Charles Laughton and Carmen Miranda were there, too. As with Monroe's mirror, these impressions are probably the result of residual energy from memorable times these people spent at the Roosevelt.

James also communicated with the spirits of lesser-known folk. He descended into the boiler room, following his theory that spirits would tend to gather near the building's energy source. He sensed a number of spirits, including one identifying himself as Ron or Ronald who claimed the room as his domain. Halfway down the steps, James distinctly felt someone slap him on the rear.

James had heard about other people's experiences with Monty Clift's spirit and wanted to spend a night in Room 928. Outside the door, James clenched his fist in response to the intensely angry energy he felt coming from the room. But at two a.m., he climbed into bed and quickly fell asleep.

Ninety minutes later, he was awakened by the sensation of a heavy weight lying across his body. Trapped and held on his side, he struggled under it, barely able to move. Slowly, he was able to draw in a deep breath and throw his arm backward. When he did, the weight lifted. It felt like a person had been lying on top of him.

Eventually, James fell back to sleep, but at 5 a.m., he awoke to see the shadow of a man seated in a chair in the corner. He would not respond to James; rather, he just sat and watched for close to thirty minutes. Then, without warning, he got up, walked toward the bathroom and disappeared. The ghost looked like Clift, and James sensed that the spirit was trapped there, unable to find peace.

Above : The pool where security guards have seen spirits take a midnight dip.

A young security guard I'll call Jerry knew nothing about ghosts when he first started at the Roosevelt—not that Jerry ever thought about ghosts. He didn't. But he does now.

"On my first night," he remembers, "I went to sleep early in an unoccupied room, so I would be alert for my 2 a.m. shift. I was awakened by someone shaking my shoulder. I turned on the light, but no one was there. I looked around the room, trying to figure out what might have happened. Finally, I went downstairs and mentioned it to security. When I asked them what they thought it might be, they just looked at each other and smiled."

Jerry experienced what he now calls the "usual stuff": feeling a presence in the hallway, especially in Clift's area; guests bolted out of their suites from the inside; calls to the switchboard from empty rooms. Then, one summer morning around three, security cameras showed a man enjoying a dip in the pool. Jerry went to check it out but saw no one. The guard at the desk told Jerry via walkie-talkie that he could clearly see a man in the shallow end. "I'm telling you," Jerry radioed back as he waved his arms through the empty air, "there's nobody here." But on the video screen, the guard saw Jerry waving his arms through the head of a man standing in the pool.

Most guests are completely unaware of ghosts at the hotel. The majority never feel a cool wind against their arms, nor do they see vanishing piano players or even Marilyn Monroe's reflection. No, most guests enjoy a peaceful stay and a touch of old Hollywood. A special few are looking for old Hollywood to touch back—those who hope to catch a glimpse of Monty Clift in Room 928. But for the most part, the Hollywood Roosevelt affords visitors a quiet look at Hollywood's past. Every once in a while, however, a guest will call the front desk to complain about noisy children playing out in the hall.

※

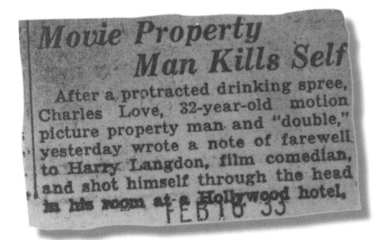

Movie Property
Man Kills Self

After a protracted drinking spree, Charles Love, 32-year-old motion picture property man and "double," yesterday wrote a note of farewell to Harry Langdon, film comedian, and shot himself through the head in his room at a Hollywood hotel,

FEB 16 33

Epilogue:

The Oban Hotel

friends to the end

*T*wo *years had passed since I had run from that ghost at the Chinese Theater. With all I'd learned since then, I hoped I would get a chance to experience another. That chance finally came at the Oban Hotel—where we may have discovered the identity of the ghost and uncovered a murder more than sixty years old in the process. When we asked the ghost, it created a big stink ... literally.*

In the 1930s, the Oban was one of many transient hotels built to accommodate the flood of hopefuls pouring into Hollywood with big dreams and little money. In the '40s, when greats like Glenn Miller and Harry James brought their big bands to the nearby Palladium or Palace, the Oban supplied perfect accommodations—clean, decent and cheap. Over the years, Clark Gable, Marilyn Monroe, James Dean and even Orson Welles reportedly made this a stop on the road to fame.

I'd passed the Oban hundreds of times, just north of Hollywood Boulevard near Vine Street, but knew nothing about it. When Marc said it might be haunted, I went there to investigate.

....

Facing Page: Is Charles Love the ghost in the basement?

"You want to know about ghosts at the Oban? Come with me." I warily followed owner Eric Eisenberg down the front hall to the back stairway. He climbed a few steps to the landing, turned and motioned for me to follow. "Stand right here," he told me, "relax, be quiet and tell me what you feel." Closing my eyes to any distractions, I began to feel a cool breeze on my calves from an open window on the landing, but there was an icy chill underneath. Slowly, I became aware of that chill all around me. The breeze had a distinctly different feel; it was cool, not cold, and it pushed against me. "This is a cold spot!" I said, opening my eyes.

"It's more than that," countered Eric. "Don't you feel it? Don't you feel them walking through you? They walk up and down these stairs all day long."

"Ghosts are walking through me right now?" I wished I felt something more ... tangible. I stepped back a few feet and felt a distinct rise in temperature. Though Eric has never seen any ghosts on the landing, he has had strong impressions about them. He feels a steady stream, a parade of spirits from the 1930s on the stairs during the day, when the hotel is active. He believes they are seeking recognition. Why else would they be out with people in the light of day? I stood in the cold spot again. Ghosts were walking through me.

"There's another ghost in the basement," Eric said. "It's a man. I've seen him. But we're doing some construction down there, and I can't take you down." I was working with a local news crew on a Haunted Hollywood segment and asked permission to return with them, plus a psychic and a few parapsychologists. Eric felt the spirits would be delighted. "Perhaps this is the recognition they've been waiting for."

Before our appointed return, Marc discovered that a man, Charles Love, had killed himself in the hotel in February of 1933. Love, thirty-three, was a prop man and double for comedian Harry Langdon. The brief story in the *Los Angeles Times* stated that after a protracted drinking spree, Love wrote a note, then shot himself in his room.

Facing Page: The ghosts at the Oban made a big stink about our visit . . . literally.

Perhaps this was the man in the basement. I shared the discovery with psychic Eddie Crispell. The night before we went to the news shoot, she called me to discuss some strong impressions she was having.

"I feel we'll find the spirit of a woman at the hotel," Eddie said. "She died there of some kind of respiratory problem. I'm also getting a strong sense that Charles Love did not commit suicide. I believe he was murdered." Perhaps that's why his spirit remains earthbound; he's seeking justice.

I arrived at the Oban at 10:30 on the appointed morning. Eddie had gotten there first and had gone immediately to the basement with Eric. "The spirit knew we were coming," Eddie informed me. "He was waiting for us at the top of the stairs." Eric confirmed that he, too, was almost knocked back by the presence as soon as he opened the basement door. Eddie showed Eric that all the hair on her arms and neck was standing up—a reaction to a presence that parapsychologists call pilo-erection.

But that wasn't all. Eddie felt the presence of another male spirit—a former owner of the hotel—on the steps above the basement where Eric had first taken me. In fact, she felt the two male spirits were by the back stairs and in the basement. "I've never seen any ghost other than the one in the basement," Eric said, "but I am open to the possibility that there are more, because I feel so much energy here."

Eddie and I descended the narrow stairway to the basement, a small, dingy room with a washer and dryer, a hot-water heater and a tiny bathroom—nothing remarkable. This was where I hoped to meet Charles Love. "This is Laurie," Eddie said out loud to the spirit. Then she turned to me. "He's right here, on this platform. Can you feel him?" I moved close to the platform, but to my consternation, I felt absolutely nothing. Eddie showed me her arm. Every hair was standing on end. On me—nothing.

"We're going to be coming back with several more people and a camera," Eddie told the spirit. "No one is going to try to make you leave. You have permission to remain here for as long as you like. We would just like to talk to you. I know it's been reported that you committed suicide, but I don't believe that. I believe you were murdered. If I'm right, when we return, please give us a physical sign—knock something over, fiddle with the lights—but please let me know if I'm right." We retired to the lobby.

Bryan Hileman, the young director of L.A.'s KTLA-TV morning news, had arrived with his camera operator; so had parapsychologist Barry Taff and his partners Barry Conrad and Jeanette Batton. Hileman interviewed Taff in the hallway for ten minutes, then we headed for the basement.

As we descended the staircase and jammed into the little room, we noticed a terrible, foul smell. Taff thought it smelled like methane gas. He covered his nose and ran out, about to be sick. Batton thought someone had vomited. We searched the room and the bathroom, but could not find the source of the odor.

Hileman proceeded to interview Eric on camera. "Twenty-five years ago, I was introduced to something down here—some sort of presence made itself known to me. It was right here where we are now that I first saw it, and where I've seen it a few times since." Eric was about ten at the time and was delivering groceries in the neighborhood.

One day, after a delivery to the hotel, he went to the basement to play. Slowly, he began to feel that he was not alone. Eric looked up. In the corner was a hazy body, a shadowy figure that seemed to shift from black to brown to rust. He sensed the figure was a man, but could not see any features or even any clothes, just the shadow. Though he had

Facing Page: Psychic Eddie Crispell and parapsychologist Dr. Barry Taff.

never encountered anything like it before, Eric knew instantly what it was. Still, he wasn't scared. He felt some sensation of contentment emanating from the figure. He and the ghost looked at each other for more than a minute before Eric scrambled up the stairs. He didn't go back to the basement for a long, long time. Years later, Eric discovered that his brother had had a similar experience. Both boys were afraid to talk about it at the time.

"I was away from the building for fifteen or twenty years," Eric told the news crew. "Nine years ago, I came to own this building, and at that time, I noticed that the feeling and the shadowy figure were still here." By the time Eric finished speaking—four or five minutes—the vile odor had left the closed, unventilated room.

On the second floor, Eddie felt the presence of the "lady ghost" she mentioned the night before. "She is not aware of the two male ghosts that inhabit the other area. They are together most of the time, but for some reason, she doesn't leave the second floor. She can't find the way out. She sticks very close to the room in which she died, near the front of the hotel. I feel she was married to the man who owned the hotel. After he died, she stayed on and died a natural death caused by a terrible lung infection, maybe tuberculosis."

We all stood on the balcony of the Oban for a time, looking out to the Hollywood Hills while we discussed the events. I felt exhilarated; Eddie had picked up on so much, and, of course, there was the vile odor that came and went so quickly. Something had happened. Eddie interpreted the odor as the sign she had asked for, that Charles Love was telling us he'd been murdered. "I've worked with the police," Jeanette said, "and I've smelled everything—chemicals, drugs, corpses. I've never smelled anything like that."

"They do that," Barry Conrad said. "Smells are something spirits do." We were all convinced something had happened.

Eric told us that over the years he has tried to communicate with the ghost in a number of ways. "It's the only ghost I've ever seen. I want to know as much about him as I can." But he has never spoken, nor will he materialize when Eric asks him.

"Eric has grown fond of the ghost over all these years of knowing him, living with him," Eddie said. "He feels no danger, and in turn, the ghost feels quite safe here. As a matter of fact, I feel that even if the truth happened to come out about his death, he would choose to remain here. I think the ghost deliberately made his presence known today so as not to discredit Eric."

"I think so, too," said Eric.

After all, I reasoned, what are old friends for?

※

bibliography

Alleman, Richard
*The Movie Lover's Guide to
Hollywood*
Harper and Row, 1985

Chaplin, Charles
My Autobiography
Simon & Schuster, 1964

Farr, Louise
*Rise and Fall of the Last
Gossip Queen*
Los Angeles Magazine,
December, 1993

Holzer, Hans
*Elvis Speaks From Beyond the Grave
and Other Celebrity Ghost Stories*
Dorset Press, 1993

Holzer, Hans
Haunted Hollywood
Bobbs-Merrill Co., 1974

Illingworth, Hal
Hotel With A Ghostly Past
Los Angeles Herald-Examiner
California Living
June 25, 1972

**Kingston, Kenny and
Marshall, Brenda**
Sweet Spirits
Contemporary Books, 1978

Kleiner, Dick
ESP and the Stars
Grosset and Dunlap, 1970

**Steiger, Sherry Hansen
and Steiger, Brad**
Hollywood and the Supernatural
St. Martin's Press, 1990

about the authors

Since the publication of her first book, *Hollywood Heartbreak*, in 1984, Laurie Jacobson has been a recognized Hollywood historian. She lives in Hollywood, where she is a writer and producer of film and television.

Marc Wanamaker, a native Angelino, is a world authority on the motion picture industry and Southern California. In 1971, he formed Bison Archives, an informational and photographic archive providing an invaluable source for films, documentaries, books, studios, museums, libraries and historical societies.